Teal, Teal Flint
Surviving Adolescence
A YOUNG ADULT NOVEL

Catina Noble

crowecreations.ca
Not Just Me © 2018; Not Again © 2019; This Is It © 2019,
Catina Noble
First Crowe Creations Print Publications

Rebranded as:
Teal, Teal Flint: Surviving Adolescence © 2023 Catina Noble
First Crowe Creations Print Publication July 2023

No part of this book may be reproduced or transmitted in any form or by any means, electronic or mechanical, including photocopying, recording, electronic transmission, or by any storage and retrieval system, without written permission from the author.
Any resemblance to persons living or dead is a coincidence.

Cover photo iStock
Cover Design © 2023 Crowe Creations
Interior design by Crowe Creations
Text set in Times New Roman; headings in Bedrock

Crowe Creations
ISBN: 978-1-998831-19-7

To Katey.

I was a teenager once too.—The real Miss Tate

Not Just Me

"The novel's beautiful message of encouragement reminds us all that no matter how challenging life may get, we can always find a silver lining in the end."—Amy MacDonald, STAR Program Supervisor, Christie Lake Kids

"Catina Noble has written a coming-of-age novel full of honesty, heart and humour. The dialogue is sharp, and skilfully captures the angst and confusion of the teenage years."—Sara Dwyer, Executive Director, Russell Heights Community House

"In *Not Just Me*, fifteen-year-old Teal Flint suffers through too many losses, both imagined and real, triggering powerful self-doubts and a profound mistrust all around her."—Phyllis Bohonis, Romantic Suspense Author, including *The Track*

Not Just Me "… carries the true, honest voice of a fifteen-year-old girl, Teal Flint, as she navigates the complexities of family life, school and growing up. Catina captures both the anguish and the joy of a sensitive young woman's life—her moods are as variable as the wind, with hope always underlying."— Heather Swail, Intermediate Teacher, ISST, Vincent Massey Public School

Not Again

Not Again continues this very real rollercoaster ride of emotions for main character, Teal. Now that she has aged, life's obstacles continue to get more and more complex. Catina Noble's writing is relatable for young adults navigating their way through the complicated teenage years, while providing suspense and entertainment for her readers."— Amy MacDonald, STAR Program Supervisor, Christie Lake Kids

"Teal is the kind of character that leaves a lasting impression, and I thought about her quite a bit after finishing her story. A brave and open-minded young woman stepping carefully through her formative years, not knowing exactly what being right means, but trusting her heart and making decisions based on her own happiness. If only I had been as grounded as Teal when I was her age! And that name, what a delight to say out loud. I despise trendy names but Teal, this I can allow, especially when it suits her so well."—Joanne MacGregor, Director of STAR Inner City Programs, Christie Lake Kids

This Is It

Review by Dakota Morgan, age 13: "When Teal graduates, she has to set down her roots and make many hard decisions about her future. Teal's friend Olive has some tough choices to make with her boyfriend. Teal is getting used to having a new stepbrother and getting along very well with Toby, and her second family. She goes on her visit to unlock some new doors in Spain with the key Miss Tate's cousin Dottie had sent to her mother. This book is very interesting and parts of it were a little scary, but I loved THIS IS IT."

Not Just Me

1

Her name was Teal. It wasn't meant for anything special. Not really, it was just her given name. The birth certificate read, Teal Flint. Apparently, her mom just really liked the color. In fact, she painted the whole house in teal. Try explaining that when company visited. Not that Teal ever had much company, but still the color was in the kitchen, the laundry room, living room and in her mom's room. It was kind of creepy. Teal supposed she should be grateful at least that she was allowed to choose the paint color for her own bedroom. Her mom was cool most of the time.

Teal's room was purple. According to many self-help sites listed on the Internet, purple represented hope and the promise of a better tomorrow. Teal had found out recently that the Internet was not always truthful. Many things could not be taken at face value. Why put up fake information for everyone to read and practice? It seemed to Teal it would make a lot more sense to write only the truth. Her mom always said "Sometimes common sense wasn't so common."

Teal wished she were a couple of inches taller. She was fifteen years old and decent looking but she was only five-foot three with boring, muddy brown hair that fell just past her shoulders, and hazel-green eyes that she felt were her best feature. Teal believed she was a little bit chunky because the scale said she weighed a hundred and thirty-five pounds. Although, the scale lied sometimes, just to upset her. Of course the number on the scale depended on how many cookies and poutines had attacked her while they screamed "Eat me!" What was a girl to do? Sometimes it was just a matter of choosing our own battles.

***

Sometimes Teal found it hard simply being Teal. Everyone said the teen years were the absolute best because you got more freedom to do the things you actually wanted to do. The sky was the limit they all said. What everyone failed to mention was, you were expected to make fewer mistakes. When mistakes were made, covering them up with a laundry basket, forging a signature, spreading a rumor or trying to reveal true feelings that just crept up, were no longer cute and acceptable. Apparently, only innocent children could do these things and get away with them.

The not-so-good things about being a teen totally crossed out the good. Therefore, in a way, Teal did not believe any of us (especially herself) were any further ahead. There were always so many things going on. She could never find the time to breathe or ask important questions, such as "when will this feeling or crisis pass?" in between messes. One thing after another drip drip dripped into her cup even when there wasn't any more room.

Teal's teacup had reached full capacity about a year earlier. Thinking back, it was probably around the same time her parents had told her they were getting a divorce. Now everything that touched her spilled over. Life was complicated.

***

Teal, her mom, and their dog, Piper, lived on the third floor of an okay apartment building located only a few blocks from downtown Ottawa. This was great because tourists always flocked to the downtown area. There were always lots of events that popped up, like Canada Day fireworks, the light-show during the winter, protests (except, a recent experience had taught Teal that it was important to find out what the protest was about before she decided to join), outdoor yoga classes, the buskers' festival, homeless people asking for money, starving artists promoting and selling their goods… There was always something going on. Kind of like her life but not nearly as much fun.

There were many interesting shops around Teal's building. There was a tiny store called Books, where you could buy used books. The whole store could fit into Teal's bedroom. She didn't think the store had a totally original name though. There was also a bakery that sold yummy chocolate croissants, a flower shop, and Karen's Coffee. There were a few other places, but these were the ones Teal liked.

The neighborhood was great for when Teal took Piper for a walk. People were friendly. Most of the shop owners left out little bowls of water for pets during the summer. Kids loved petting Piper, almost as much as the elderly did.

The truth was that Piper and Teal were best friends. She had a human best friend but her dog was the bestest best friend. Just don't tell Teal's friend Olive. Piper never made fun of Teal or hurt her feelings. He was the perfect kind of best friend. In addition, he had yet to start a rumor and he always believed her.

Piper was three years old and weighed just over five pounds. He was a little dog that Teal could carry around in her arms, although her mom constantly reminded her that Piper could walk by himself without any help. Teal knew that, she just felt cool when she carried him around. Piper was very cute. Everyone said so. Even Miss Tate—who didn't like dogs, cats, or anyone else for that matter—said so. This counted for something. Anyway, it was all the proof Teal needed.

Miss Tate was Teal's grumpy next-door neighbor. Teal didn't know why Miss Tate never seemed happy. Teal didn't understand her. Sometimes she thought Miss Tate felt lost and alone. If this was true, she could completely relate. She felt the same way sometimes. Other people just didn't get it. It was strange to feel alone and lost when people were around her. She had her mom, her dad, Piper and Olive, but sometimes Teal still felt alone.

She hated feeling like that and it drove her crazy.

Teal sighed as her stomach growled. She rummaged through her backpack for the third time. Her house key had to be somewhere. She yanked things out of the bag in frustration and tossed them onto the corridor's floor beside her. She had no idea when her mom would be home. Her cell phone was dead, and the charger—of course—was in her room. She never had the charger when she actually needed it!

There was nowhere for Teal to go. Miss Tate had let her stay in her apartment the last time she had been locked out. That was back in January, though, when it was thirty degrees below zero. The wind had been so strong, the news channel had even issued a snowstorm warning. That was the only reason Miss Tate had let her stay inside the apartment. Miss Tate had even made Teal a cup of tea. If the truth were known, Teal preferred pop and chips but the tea had been yummy. Who knew Teal would become a fan of tea? Teal had been with Miss Tate for about an hour before her mom got in from work.

It was nice outside today so Teal guessed she could potentially go for a walk to kill time if she couldn't find the damn key. What she really wanted was a can of pop and a few cookies to munch on until her mom got home and made supper. This wasn't looking good at all. The lack of a silly key was currently all that stood between Teal and happiness.

Finally Teal spotted the key. Of course she found it after she'd emptied out all the crap onto the floor. She picked up her stuff and quickly threw everything back into the bag. She unlocked the door, tossed the bag on the kitchen table, and spotted a note.

> *Teal,*
> *A reminder.*
> *You are visiting your dad tomorrow.*
> *Love,*
> *Mom*

2

TEAL ROLLED HER EYES OUT OF HABIT. Every time she did this, it apparently "insulted" her mom.

Her mother found the gesture rude. However, it wasn't as though Teal did it on purpose. That thought made her flinch. Maybe that was not completely true. Sometimes Teal did roll her eyes on purpose but not all the time! Teal was such a great kid, her mom had to find a reason to complain.

Teal ripped up the note and tossed the scraps of paper into the garbage. She usually visited her dad every weekend so how could she possibly forget? "Seriously, Mom, sometimes you just have too much time on your hands." She voiced her frustration to the empty room.

Of course, Teal hadn't forgotten she was going to her father's. It had been a year since the divorce but she still struggled with it. She knew her mother was happier now that he was gone. Her father didn't seem to care about the whole situation either way. He had a two-bedroom apartment so she even had her own room when she went over to visit.

He lived fifteen blocks away. Whenever Teal slept over, they would make chocolate chip pancakes together in the morning. He always poured butter-flavored syrup all over the pancakes. They used so much syrup it was almost as if the pancakes were mini floating devices. She smiled just thinking about making pancakes with her father again over the weekend.

Teal left her cell in her room to charge. She was sure Olive would send a text later to let her know if she had met up with her boyfriend after all.

Olive was Teal's best friend. Olive was skinny, five foot six and about a hundred and fifteen pounds. Olive was beautiful. The first thing Teal had noticed about her when they first met was her jet-black hair that fell straight down to the waist and her piercing blue eyes. If Teal had great hair and seductive blue eyes, she would also have a boyfriend.

Olive's real name was Olivia, but she really hated it when anyone called her that. Teal dared anyone to call her Olivia to her face just to see what would happen. Olive would probably punch them hard in the arm just to make sure they didn't do it again. Everyone called her Olive.

They had been friends ever since the first day of kindergarten and had always been lucky enough to be in the same classes. This year sucked; they weren't in any of the same grade ten courses. What sucked even more was that Olive's boyfriend, Brad, was in almost all of Teal's classes. She didn't like Brad.

Olive and Brad had only been together for two weeks, but Olive made Teal spy on him all the time. Brad seemed nice enough but Teal didn't feel comfortable around him. It was creepy how he would always stare a little too long at all the girls, and that included Teal. What was his problem? She wondered if Olive ever realized that Teal had better things to do with her time than spy on her boyfriend. Teal did have a life of her own. Not as much as Olive, though. Olive had Brad.

Teal checked the pantry to see what they had. The cookie selection looked slim. She grabbed the chocolate-chip cookies; oatmeal didn't appeal to her. She grabbed a can of pop to go with the cookies and headed for the living room.

She wanted a TV in her room but her mother didn't think it was a good idea. Teal's mom believed if she got one that it would distract Teal from school work and other things. What other things? *Yeah right.* All of Teal's friends had TVs in their rooms.

"What are you worried about, Mom? Are you afraid I won't leave my room if I had a TV?"

The empty room didn't answer. okay, maybe her mother was on to something.

Teal checked the time on the DVD player. It was a few minutes before 4:00, time for her favorite show, *Criminal Minds*. If she watched a bit of action with Shemar Moore, it might lift her spirits. She decided she'd take what she could get.

Teal heard her mother's voice as she walked toward her bedroom. "Hi Teal, how was your day?"

Teal blamed her height on her mom who was five foot exactly and weighed a hundred pounds but only when she was soaking wet. She couldn't blame her hair on her mother because her mother had strawberry blonde hair that she cut short, just below the jaw line. Their eyes were identical, though. They both had hazel-green. As soon as her mother got home, she always changed into her pajamas. Her mother said wearing regular clothes made her uncomfortable.

"It was okay. What about you? Any crazy customers today?" Teal asked before the door to her mom's room closed.

Her mom worked at a pharmacy and dispensed medication. Every so often, a customer would come in and complain about the cost of the medication or the cost of the standard dispensing fee. Like this was her mother's fault. They didn't have to shop where her mother worked. They were welcome to shop anywhere else. Teal guessed her mother wasn't the only person with too much time on their hands.

Her mom came back out wearing cute pj's with cupcakes printed all over them. "No crazies today. I thought we'd order in a veggie pizza for supper. Is that good?"

It didn't bother Teal most of the time that her mom was a vegetarian. Nevertheless, for certain things, meat was a must. For Teal, this included pizza. She considered eating pizza without meat "unnatural." It was like going to the movies and not buying any popcorn. "What was even the point in going to the movies?" she wondered.

"Sure, a veggie pizza sounds perfect with bacon and

hamburger crumble on my half." Teal couldn't help but smile.

She looked around the living from for the cordless phone, finally spotting it on the armchair, right beside Piper.

He was lounging on the La-Z-Boy as he quietly watched every move her mom made. It was as if he were afraid to close his eyes in case he missed something important. He had a lot of time to spare. After *Criminal Minds* ended, Teal decided to take Piper out for a quick walk around the block.

***

When Teal got back, she headed straight to her bedroom to check her cell. She had two new messages. One was from her father and the other was from Olive.

She checked Olive's message first. Best friends came before parents, always.

> Brad is late and hasn't returned my text. What should I do?-O

Teal knew Olive. If Teal was late by even one minute, Olive stretched out the truth. No matter how little or long she waited, to Olive it always seemed like forever.

The message from her father said he had a surprise and was looking forward to seeing her tomorrow.

Teal smiled thinking it would be funny if the surprise was a TV for her bedroom at her mom's.

Teal responded to Olive.

> Seriously, how long have you been waiting for him?-T

> Fifteen minutes.-O

Olive had replied before Teal even had the chance to put her cell back down.

Logically thinking, if Olive hadn't heard from Brad, maybe he'd forgotten or something.

> Wait another fifteen minutes. Maybe something came up or his cell died.-T

> KK.-O

The doorbell rang and she heard her mother chatting up the delivery person while she paid for the food.

Teal placed her cell phone on a side table in the living room. Her mother hated it when she had her cell out while they ate supper. Her mother thought it was rude. Her mother seemed to have a whole list of stuff Teal did that she considered rude. Teal thought her mother needed to get a hobby. Her mother was the only one who thought her rude… At least she was the only one who said it to Teal's face. In Teal's world, something wasn't considered true just because one person thought it was.

Teal and her mother made small talk while they each grabbed two slices of pizza. Teal mentioned the note her mom had left and said she planned on going to her dad's.

Teal decided not mention the surprise. If she did get the TV, her mom would be caught off guard! Teal was already thinking about the look on her mom's face! In Teal's mind, the TV was already in her room and she had Shemar Moore completely at her disposal.

Out of the blue, her mother asked about Olive.

Teal rambled on about Olive's new boyfriend, but her mother furrowed her eyebrows more and more as Teal kept talking. Teal paused in the middle of a sentence to study her reaction.

"Teal, you and Olive are too young to date. Not until you have finished school." This was not the first time she'd given Teal this lecture.

Teal wondered why she was the one getting the lecture. Olive was the one with the boyfriend. As if, anyone would be interested in Teal. Obviously her mother didn't know how things worked in the real world. Or at least in Teal's world.

"Actually, make that no dating until you are twenty-two." Her mother nodded to herself. Her mother was the parent, not Teal. This was already understood.

Teal had heard this lecture many times before so she rolled her eyes in response. She smiled as her mother glared. Teal bit her tongue and decided it was best not to say a word back because this would be considered "rude." The truth was, Teal wanted to tell her mother that glaring at people (like her mom was doing) was also rude.

When her mother had asked about the guy Olive was seeing, she had stopped as soon as she heard the name Brad. As in she put-the-pizza-down-and-stopped-chewing kind of stopped.

"What?" Teal shrugged. *What was her problem?*

"Is his name Brad Trenton? The guy who plays football at your school?"

Her mother waited for a reply, but she never looked away from Teal. It was kind of creepy from where Teal sat. In fact, her mother reminded Teal of Brad himself right now.

"Yeah. Why?" Her thoughts were racing. *Why did her mom care so much about the guy Olive was dating? What was in it for her? Olive was dating him and Olive was Teal's best friend. So of course Teal was in it but she didn't see how it was any of her mom's business.*

Teal licked the last hint of pizza sauce off her right thumb.

"Are you sure it's Brad Trenton, that football kid in your class?"

Teal looked at her mother. Had the woman lost her hearing while Teal was at school? On the other hand, was she deliberately trying to piss Teal off? What was her problem?

"Yes, Mom, Olive is with Brad Trenton." Teal repeated this slowly for effect as she waited for something dramatic to take place. After a couple of moments, nothing happened and now Teal felt stupid.

"Oh." Her mother picked up the dirty dishes and carried them over to the dishwasher.

"What?" Teal asked in frustration. She hadn't been given any indication as to why her mother was asking these questions when Olive was not her daughter.

Maybe her mother thought it was not right for Olive to date anyone at all in her book. Maybe Brad had nothing to do with it.

Teal stared as her mother wiped down the kitchen counter and the table with a teal-colored dishcloth. Her mother looked deep in thought.

"I saw Trina with Brad at the mall around lunch time.

The two of them were holding hands." Her mother's voice was barely above a whisper. Her eyes locked with Teal's.

Teal took a long swig from her can of pop. She needed a moment. She had to say something. Anything really, just so she didn't feel stupid. Olive was her best friend and of course she felt the need to defend her because that's what best friends did. That was part of the friendship code.

Teal's mother stared and waited.

"You saw them?" Teal asked even though no amount of confirmation would satisfy her.

Her mother was quiet.

Brad was with Trina, holding hands, while he was currently dating her best friend, Olive.

Teal smiled. She was jealous of Olive because she had a boyfriend and she didn't. In addition, Olive was beautiful. Teal's smile quickly faded. This was serious. What if her mother had made this whole thing up to convince Teal that dating was not such a good idea?

Teal thought about it for a moment. No way. Her mother would never do something like that.

"I have homework to do," was the only response Teal could manage. There was nothing left to say.

Teal grabbed her phone and made her way to her room to figure out what to do. She wanted to see if Olive had, in fact, met up with Brad.

There was a text from Olive.

> Waited for over an hour for Brad at our usual coffee place. He never showed up.

> Now I'm grounded because I forgot to call Mom and let her know that I had plans after school.
>
> She is taking my cell away right after I send this text. No cell for a week!-O

This was actually a relief to Teal. She needed time to decide what to do and if Olive didn't have her phone, she wouldn't expect a reply back. Brad was six feet tall, well-muscled, about one hundred and eighty pounds; his dark brown hair was always kept super short like a crew cut. His eyes were the color of chocolate. Yes, he was good-looking, but Teal still didn't like him. The next time she would speak to or see Olive wouldn't be until Monday morning when they grabbed their stuff from their lockers before class started. This was great! Teal had some time to think.

3

Teal heard the alarm go off. It was already ten a.m. It was time to get up and get ready to go see her father. She was cozy and didn't want to move.

Then she remembered that he had a surprise for her. A smile pulled at the corners of her mouth. She slowly peeled back the cover and eventually made her way to the bathroom.

After that chore was done, Teal added her journal to her backpack. She was sure she had everything she needed to spend the night. Her mother had already left for yoga class. Teal grabbed a fresh sticky note from the stash on top of the fridge.

Have a good day!

She added a happy face to the note before she stuck it to the fridge. Her mom would see it when she reached for her yogurt. Her mother always had one cup of yogurt after yoga class to cool down.

Before Teal left the kitchen, she put a pee-pad down on the floor for Piper. She kissed him as she passed by, but he didn't even move. Piper was the only one who used the La-Z-Boy.

She grabbed her bag and headed out the door.

Just as Teal was double-checking to make sure the door was locked, Miss Tate appeared in the hallway.

Teal raised her eyebrows as Miss Tate glared.

Even though Miss Tate was about the same height and weight as her mother, the woman's deep sea-green eyes frightened Teal when she glared. Miss Tate's white hair was always pulled back into a tight bun.

Maybe that was why Miss Tate was always grumpy. She needed to let her hair down. *What is her problem?* She didn't have to go to school or work, walk a dog or miss her favorite TV shows. She could do whatever she wanted. If Teal could do whatever she wanted, she would be happy, that was for sure.

Miss Tate didn't say word.

Suddenly, Teal felt bad. Miss Tate lived all alone and didn't have any pets. Teal wasn't even sure if she had ever been married or whether she had kids or grandkids. She didn't think so though. Teal never saw anyone visiting Miss Tate and neither had her mother. Not even during the holidays.

Teal was in a great mood. She was on her way to her father's and he had a surprise for her. Against her better judgment, she decided to stop and talk with Miss Tate.

Teal was a good person for doing this and she knew it.

"How are you today, Miss Tate?" Teal offered a smile. She was proud of herself. Her mother would be impressed with her for sure.

"Alive." Miss Tate spat out the words, as she glared.

Teal felt uncomfortable and her smile quickly disappeared. What did she mean by her reply? Teal was just about to ask when Miss Tate stepped back inside the apartment and slammed the door. If her mother had been with her, she would have called that rude for sure.

Teal vowed that the next time she spotted the older woman, she would keep quiet. She had been in a great mood, had gone out of her way to talk to her and now she felt stupid.

She had to shake off the mood and focus on something else. Teal played a small game as she walked. She checked out all the little shops on her way to her father's apartment. The bakery shops with the chocolate pastries were the best ones. *Never trust anyone who doesn't like chocolate.* That was definitely a Life and Friend code.

Teal tried not to step on the cracks on the sidewalks. When she and Olive were younger, they would hold hands and avoid every single crack they came across. They would do this as they chanted "Step on a crack and break your mother's back." It used to drive her mother crazy. Not because it was rude—although yelling at the top of their lungs was fun, not that other people found it entertaining—but because it would take them three times as long to get to where they were going.

Then Teal thought of Olive. She wondered what she was doing right at this moment. It was out of Teal's hands though. She would have to wait to talk to her.

***

Teal arrived at her father's building and pressed his buzzer number, one-zero-one, and waited. After three beeps, she could walk in.

She walked through the entrance lobby and quickly turned left. She could already taste the chocolate pancakes. She had her own key to his apartment, but didn't like using it because it just felt weird. She knocked on the door using their special knock, a quick three taps.

Her father swung open the door and held out his arms for their usual bear hug. It felt great to be in his arms. He was six foot two with short dark hair and weighed about two hundred and twenty pounds. Hugging her dad was like hugging a life-sized teddy bear. He smelled good. It was more than just after-shave. Maybe he was wearing some sort of cologne. She smiled thinking about it. It was nice of him to put in so much effort just for her. Sometimes her father really was thoughtful.

Teal's father was cool. She knew she really was lucky to have such amazing parents. She could have a pain-in-the-ass mother like Olive's was. Olive had had her cell phone taken away just because she'd forgotten to call and check in! Teal's mother would never do that to her. Her mother would have given her a lecture on how worried she'd been thinking that Teal had possibly been abducted by aliens or recruited into a prostitution ring. After the lecture, Teal would have rolled her eyes and that would have been the end of it. Seriously, let the punishment fit the crime. No wonder Olive and her mother didn't have the best relationship.

Teal walked into the living room and stopped in her tracks. She couldn't move or speak. Sitting on the couch right there was a pretty woman with dark, curly hair and pink glasses.

Teal's father walked up beside the woman and placed his left hand on her shoulder and smiled. Like they were best friends or something.

"Teal, this is Tonya."

The woman stood at the sound of her name and offered her hand to Teal to shake.

Teal looked her up and down. Tonya was wearing heels but it was obvious she was taller than Teal. Tonya's hair came down to her shoulders and the pink glasses appeared to be neon against her pale-blue eyes. Physically, Tonya was the complete opposite of Teal's mother. Nevertheless, if Tonya had looked like her mother, she knew it would still bother her. Maybe Teal wasn't over the divorce after all.

"Your dad has talked about you so much, I feel as though I know you already." She smiled brightly.

Teal stood in silence. *Who is this Tonya chick?*

She just couldn't help herself and blurted out,

"Dad has never said a single word about you," *Hey, it was the truth.*

Tonya turned and looked directly at Teal's father. "Danny? You didn't tell her you had a girlfriend?"

Teal's jaw actually dropped as she heard that awful word: *girlfriend*. A moment of panic seized her. She wondered what was going on. All Teal wanted to do was spend time with her father. She wanted to make chocolate-chip pancakes. Olive had Brad. Yeah, he was a jerk but at least she had a boyfriend. All Teal had was chocolate-chip pancakes with her father and only on the weekends.

Teal wished she could disappear into a hole in the floor. She waited to see if her wish would be granted but nothing happened. The floor didn't magically swallow her up. She was on her own with another mess as usual. Teal was always on her own.

Her father replied, "Tonya is going to spend the afternoon with us so she can get to know you better."

Note to self: Her father had not denied the fact that Tonya was his girlfriend. This confirmed that Tonya was in fact her father's girlfriend. Therefore, this was why he smelled so good?

It had nothing to do with me at all. Her father had done all of this for Tonya, his girlfriend. *What a mess!*

Teal was angry. Her thoughts turned to her best friend. It was just like Olive to go and get herself grounded from her cell phone at a time when Teal needed her.

What was Teal going to do? She couldn't just leave her father with Tonya. That would be dangerous. She knew how other women could be. Tonya would wrap her father around her little finger. Besides, as her mother would say, it would be rude to leave on the spot like that.

It was only an hour into the visit and Teal already wished she was back at her mother's. Staying had been a mistake.

Tonya kept smiling at her and talking about how much fun they were going to have with Toby.

Teal had pieced together that Toby was her cat. Toby

was three years old. *Whoop-de-doo!* She cared nothing for cats. She was a dog person. And Teal was certain there was a saying about not trusting people who didn't like dogs. Tonya hadn't exactly said that, but she did have a cat instead of a dog. That was a fact. It was also pretty much the same thing.

During supper, Tonya had sent three texts. Three! Teal's father hadn't said a word about how rude it was to text at the table. Maybe her father and mother were not going to get back together after all.

Teal told Tonya about Piper who was also three years old. Who knew, maybe Toby and Piper could get together for some sort of play date. Teal told Tonya this would be a brilliant idea. Teal thought she was being very mature. Her mother would be proud of her. Teal had made an effort.

After supper, Teal went to her room. She wanted to write in her journal and vent about the day. What she really needed to do was to talk to Olive, but Olive was not available to Teal in her time of need. Teal felt this was unfair. She had always been there for Olive no matter what.

4

UGH. THIS SUCKED BIG TIME. Teal's thoughts ran rampant. There had better be chocolate-chip pancakes in the morning or else things just might get ugly. No pancakes with her father would be the last straw. She wasn't sure how much more of this she could take. She had just started getting used to the fact that her dad was gone and now he was with someone else? Too much drama. As she drifted off to sleep, a single tear slid down Teal's left cheek and fell onto her pillow. Growing up wasn't all it was cracked up to be.

Teal opened her eyes and checked her cell. It was 9:00 a.m., the time they usually started making the pancakes together.

By 9:30 a.m. they were enjoying them with a hot beverage. Usually, they had hot chocolate but occasionally her father would make a mixture of random stuff and then they would laugh for weeks about his latest experiment. She wondered if Tonya was still there.

Last night Teal's father had knocked on her door to say goodnight. She hadn't bothered to invite him in. She hadn't been ready to talk about the whole situation. She had no idea if Miss Tonya would be joining them for breakfast. She wasn't sure she liked surprises anymore either. Her definition of a surprise was something fun and something you actually liked.

Teal tentatively took a step into the kitchen. She was on guard for the next mess that surely waited for her. Her father was at the kitchen counter, mixing the batter for the pancakes. She walked up and gave him a big hug and decided to get her question out of the way. She thought it best to be prepared just in case.

"Will Tonya be sharing the pancakes with us?" Teal remained casual and looked down at the floor as she walked to the fridge to busy herself with the task of locating the bag of chocolate-chips for the batter.

"Tonya went home last night. I thought meeting her for the first time was enough for now." Her father gave the batter one last whirl before pouring the mixture onto the griddle.

Teal sighed and smiled at the same time. Everything was all right for the moment. It was just her and her dad. It was Sunday morning and this was their usual routine. Best of all, Tonya was nowhere to be found. Teal was no longer upset with Olive for getting her phone taken away. Teal felt mature. She could handle things on her own!

She sat down and took a sip of the mint hot chocolate her father had made to go with breakfast. There were even mini marshmallows. Teal loved the mini ones. They were so cute, just the right size for so many things. The regular ones were just that: regular. The mini ones were special.

They spent the rest of the afternoon together, except for an hour, because her dad got an emergency call to fix something at a seniors' residence. He had to take it because he was the one on call for the weekend. Teal was okay with that. The pancakes were delicious, they had mini marshmallows, and there was no Tonya. Things had finally started looking up.

While her father was gone, Teal wrote in her journal and did some research on the Internet. She was thinking of getting her nose pierced. She hadn't told her mom or dad yet. She wasn't sure what her father would say. However, she was sure her mom would find it rude or offensive somehow. Her mother would take Teal's decision personally. Like what kind of mother was she because Teal decided to get her nose pierced? Why couldn't some things just be about her?

For now, Teal would keep this secret to herself. She had written about it but she hadn't even told Olive. Olive had her beauty and Brad. Teal had this. It wasn't much, but it was hers. She had always known that you have to work with what you have. Well, Teal supposed, she did have Tonya but she wasn't much to brag about so far. It was best to pretend Tonya didn't exist. At least for the moment.

5

AT SCHOOL ON MONDAY MORNING, Teal hadn't seen Olive at her locker. Where was she? Teal hadn't been in touch with her all weekend and she needed to tell her about Brad. If Olive found out that Teal knew and hadn't told her, it would be the end of their friendship for sure. Teal had seen other people wind up on Olive's bad side and knew that was a place she had no desire to be.

Of course, just as she'd secured her lock to leave, Olive showed up. Great, now they were both rushed.

"Slept in," Olive explained, shrugging like it wasn't a big deal. Teal told her she had to go but definitely needed to talk to her at lunch for real.

"Kay kay," was Olive's reply as she turned away to make her way to class.

Teal had to get through four classes before it was lunch time. She couldn't concentrate at all. She was worried how Olive would react to the news about Brad. The whole situation had been eating at her all weekend. She just had to tell her and get it over with. She worried that Olive might be just another notch on Brad's belt. It wouldn't be right.

Finally, lunch hour arrived. Just in time, as Teal's stomach had started growling.

Teal headed for their usual table in the center of the cafeteria. She arrived at the table first. This was no surprise since she practically ran to make sure she got to Olive before Brad did. Teal hoped Brad had some sports practice or might be busy chatting with his "other girlfriend." She didn't really care where Brad was, as long as it wasn't anywhere near her.

She was nervous. If Olive was in a good mood, this would destroy her. If she was in a bad mood, the news would destroy both her and Teal. Any way Teal looked at it, the news would not go over well. Sometimes it was hard being yourself. Why were things always such a mess? Was it like this for everyone? Was it just her? Olive arrived and set her bag on the table before she sat down.

Olive started first. "How did it go at your dad's place?"

Teal looked down at the pasta salad. It was no comfort to her at a time like this. A big poutine slathered with cheese curds would have been a much better choice for this nerve-racking moment. How should she tell Olive that Brad was cheating on her? What was the code for a situation like this?

"What's up, Teal? You have something to tell me?"

Teal took a deep breath in and out. She had to do it.

"On Friday, when Brad never showed up, my mom saw him with Trina at the mall. It gets worse. They were holding hands." Teal stopped breathing and dramatically clamped her hand over her mouth. She waited for Olive's reaction relieved that her part was done.

Olive was silent for a full five minutes. Teal knew this because she kept checking her cell phone for the time. She was secretly hoping to get an emergency text from her mom or her dad that would force her to have to suddenly leave. This would diffuse the situation for the pair of them. Olive and silence did not go together. The silence scared Teal. Olive wasn't the type of girl to merely sit and be quiet after hearing bad news. Not a good sign for sure. Teal was right.

Olive stood up. "Liar," she blurted out as she stomped away. She didn't even look back.

"Olive!" Teal shouted out her name, but she kept moving until she completely disappeared from the cafeteria.

Teal was too stunned to move. The worst part was knowing that Olive still didn't have access to her phone. She wouldn't be able to call Olive after she'd cooled off and digested the news. Teal reminded herself that once Olive had time to calm down and come to her senses, she would realize that Teal was a very loyal friend. Telling her had been the right thing to do.

Then why was Teal now second-guessing herself?

***

Teal arrived home, surprised to find her mother already home. This was unusual.

"Is everything okay?" Teal asked quietly.

"It's one of my silly headaches. I'm going to try to get some rest. There are leftovers in the fridge to heat up for supper."

Teal watched as her mom rubbed her temples. A minute later she got up from the couch, walked to her bedroom door and closed it.

After Teal heated up the lasagna, she rushed through her homework quickly. Once it was done, she decided to curl up with Piper on the couch and watch reruns of *Criminal Minds*.

But no matter how many episodes she watched, Teal still felt miserable. She knew Olive was angry. What if she never spoke to Teal again? What if their friendship was over for good?

Teal was on her own with Piper for the night. She flopped onto her bed and snuggled her pet.

"Maybe this is for the best, Piper. I don't want Mom to worry about me and I certainly don't want her prying into my personal matters either. Sometimes she forgets I'm a teenager. That we need our own space."

The little dog sat up and tilted his head with one ear up as if he understood every word she was saying, then licked her cheek.

Teal cried for a while before she finally fell into a fragmented sleep.

6

That night, Teal dreamed that Olive stood right in front of her. They were face to face, their eyes locked. Olive was beautiful and sexy. As Teal leaned in to kiss her lips, the alarm sounded. Teal awakened with a start.

After a few minutes, she remembered she was mad at Olive. Teal had done absolutely nothing wrong. If the roles had been switched, she would have wanted Olive to tell her. Teal was a good and loyal friend to Olive. Olive shouldn't be upset with her, she should, in fact, be upset with Brad. She couldn't get thoughts of the dream and what it might mean out her head.

Once Teal arrived at her locker, she waited as long as she could. She hoped to see Olive but Olive ended up being a no-show.

Teal arrived at first class and was immediately lost in her own thoughts. She had so much on her mind. There was the whole thing with her father and Tonya plus now the drama with Olive. Not to mention the dream. *Why was I trying to kiss her?* Nothing made sense anymore.

Teal tried to picture her life without Olive in it. The thought was completely depressing. Next, she wondered about her father and Tonya getting married. It was all too much. She shook her head. *This can't be happening.*

At lunch, Teal sat at their usual table and waited for Olive to show up. She ate a poutine and waited for the entire lunch hour but Olive never bothered to show. Every so often, Teal scanned the crowd. Finally, she gave up, stood, put her garbage away, and dropped the tray through its proper slot.

As she exited the door of the cafeteria, she spotted Brad. Then he was right in front of her.

At first Brad glared. Next, he inhaled deeply. His eyes went from glaring to bulging and his hair looked as though he had just rolled out of bed.

Teal's heart stopped. No matter how much she willed them to, her feet would not budge. She was paralyzed with fear. She was now a sitting duck.

"I am not sure what you think your mom saw at the mall. I wasn't there on Friday." He was furious.

"Oh." She knew it was an inane response but what else could she say.

"I was home sick. I strongly suggest you tell Olive you were mistaken and that you will make this up to her somehow." He glared again.

What? Was this a threat? Had he just threatened her? If he was acting this way, it only confirmed that her mother had in fact told the truth.

Teal took a step back to the left and marched right by

him. She hadn't said a word. For one, she was in shock and two, she really felt there was nothing else to say. Brad was a cheat and a jerk. This was evident. Plain and simple. He was not good enough for her Olive.

After the run-in with Brad, Teal headed to the school's office to use the phone. She called her mother at work and told her she wasn't feeling well and needed permission to leave school early.

Lucky for Teal, her mother hadn't asked why and she was allowed to leave.

Good. At least I don't have to sit around the school walking on eggshells for fear of running into Brad or Olive.

Teal quickly went to her locker and gathered her stuff. She headed for home, walking more slowly than usual. She didn't feel like being at school but then again, she didn't really like the thought of being home alone either. Teal's mind strayed back to the image of her about to kiss Olive. She tried to erase the image because that's what she felt she should do. However, part of her didn't want to.

***

Teal stood outside her apartment door with the key. She tried the lock three times but fumbled again and again. She couldn't seem to get the damn door open.

Footsteps sounded behind her.

Teal slowly turned around. It was Miss Tate.

As Miss Tate arrived at her door, she stopped and looked up. Their eyes met and Teal turned her face away. She couldn't handle Miss Tate right now.

"What's wrong, Teal?" Miss Tate asked in a soothing voice.

Teal didn't answer. She had never heard Miss Tate use this tone before. Why did she think something was wrong? What did she care anyway? Miss Tate only remembered her name because her mother signed it on the Christmas card she gave her every year.

"I'm not sure what you mean Miss Tate."

"I've been around long enough to know when something is amiss. Besides, tears are trailing down your face."

She moved closer to Teal.

"You're upset. What's bothering you, child?"

Teal raised her right hand to touch her own cheek. She was crying over some silly fight with her best friend and now her father might marry Tonya. She was pathetic. She thought again about the dream. The dream. She couldn't possibly tell anyone about the dream.

Miss Tate slowly turned Teal and guided her into her own apartment.

Teal tried to explain that she would be fine. But she was not doing a good job of convincing her. She couldn't even get a sentence out. She was a mess, and she was the only one who could clean it up. Unfortunately.

"I will make tea and we can chat. Just for a few minutes. You can tell me what this fuss is all about."

Gently, Miss Tate hugged Teal then passed a box of tissues to her.

Who is this woman?

Maybe Miss Tate had a change of heart. Teal blew her nose and tried to gain composure as their neighbor clattered around in the kitchen. Her life had come down to this. She was such a mess that she now required a chaperon. Then the stupid tears started to fall again.

Miss Tate had remembered the way Teal liked her tea from the last visit—three cream and three sugars. Teal took her first sip and closed her eyes. The tea gave her a moment to breathe. She took another deep breath and started to tell Miss Tate about the two major catastrophes in her life.

She decided to start with Olive and then went off about Tonya for a while.

Miss Tate listened, nodding her head every so often.

What am I doing? Why am I pouring my heart out to her? She is an ugly old woman who doesn't care about anyone but herself. What does she know about being a teenager? Teal noted not to tell her about the dream.

As Teal took the last sip from the cup, Miss Tate got up to refill it. It was still nice and warm. Miss Tate looked at Teal for a moment and then spoke.

"If Olive is a true friend, she will come around. Just give her time, dear. If she is not a good friend, then as much as it hurts, maybe it's time for you two to go your separate ways. Some friends are not meant to be held onto forever. Friends grow apart. I think you did the right thing by telling Olive about Brad. You are a good friend to tell her and if she can't see that, you deserve a friend who appreciates you for who you are."

Miss Tate took a long sip of her tea before she continued.

"As for your father, maybe Tonya won't be around much longer. No one ever knows how long these things might last. I know you're upset with him. He likes Tonya though. So, unless she gives you a reason not to like her, as long as she treats you with respect, you should do the same and give her a chance. Really, Teal, this is all you can do about Tonya. I may be old and set in my ways but I haven't forgotten how emotional being a teenager can be. Quite frankly, the teenage years suck."

Teal stared at Miss Tate. Maybe she wasn't crazy after all. Maybe she had been unfair in her judgment? Maybe there was more to this woman than Teal had given her credit for. The advice made sense. No matter how upset Olive was with her, she didn't regret busting Brad. In fact, she would want her to do the same thing if the shoe were on the other foot. And as for Tonya, Teal didn't really have control over who her father dated. As long as his dates were civil to her, she would have to make an effort to be nice, at least for his sake. He deserved that much from her.

Teal stayed with Miss Tate until she heard her mother unlock the apartment door. She thanked Miss Tate and left quickly. It was hard to imagine Miss Tate as a teenager, Teal stifled a laugh.

7

It was Friday morning. Teal was still trying to decide if she was going to her father's or not. She hadn't wanted to text him only to find out that Tonya would be there. She felt bad for him though. Maybe this weekend she would go over and just see what might happen. She needed to take things one weekend at a time.

Teal knew she would somehow get through the "Tonya Situation." At least she would only have to deal with her on the weekends. That wasn't so bad.

***

There were too many changes. The dream tried to surface once again but Teal refused to let it. She pushed it down so low inside it made her feel sick to her stomach.

***

Teal arrived at her locker and was surprised to see Olive on the floor sitting in front of her own locker. Her head was down and cradled in her arms. She hadn't heard Teal arrive.

Teal decided not to say anything and quietly opened her locker. Her plan was to quickly gather her stuff and walk away before Olive noticed.

However, she heard Olive quietly crying. She stopped for a second to make sure it really was Olive. Teal had heard Olive cry only a handful of times during their entire friendship.

Olive's sobs became louder. Obviously, she was upset so there was no way Teal could leave. She bent down in front of her friend and touched her on the shoulder. Olive looked up to see Teal and smiled briefly through her tears but the smile faded quickly.

Even though she was a complete mess right now, Olive still looked beautiful. Teal sat down, put her arm around her, and moved in a bit closer. Olive remained quiet. They continued to sit like this for a few more minutes.

The bell rang, letting everyone know they should now be at their first class. It was official. They were late. As if they cared. Right now, Olive needed Teal. As her friend, Teal needed to see what she could do to help. If she didn't want it, they could go their separate ways. She would have to try.

Slowly, Olive looked up at Teal and mumbled something unintelligible.

"I can't hear you when you mumble." Teal replied gently.

Olive swiped her jet-black hair out of her face. She looked straight at Teal.

"You were right. How am I ever to going to live this down? How could he do this to me?"

Teal didn't t want to ask what she meant and upset her all over again. She assumed she was talking about Brad and Trina.

"Teal. It was awful. I saw them. They kissed and they were holding hands at the food court. And to make the whole matter worse, I was with my mother. My mother saw them! I felt so stupid." Olive started to sob all over again.

Teal squeezed her. She felt sorry she had to go through this and imagined how hurt she must be but Teal was glad that Olive finally believed her. Olive now knew that Teal hadn't made up any rumors.

Just then, Principal Marcus stopped in front of them.

"Ladies, you are late for class. Go get a late slip and get to class. Now."

Mr. Marcus had been around for over a decade. Teal bit her tongue. What she really wanted to say was "Thanks, Mr. Obvious."

All of the students had heard the stories. The bottom line was that none of the students ever questioned Principal Marcus. Students always did what they were told no matter what. So Olive and Teal remained silent. They stood up together and they walked toward the office to get a slip.

With slip in hand, Teal hugged Olive and told her to hang in there. Things seemed crummy now but in a couple more days, hopefully, she would start feeling better. Brad was a jerk. Olive didn't need someone like him around. Teal told Olive she would see her in the usual spot at the caf at lunch. Olive nodded but didn't reply.

At Teal's next class, she couldn't concentrate. She was worried about Olive and the dream. What had happened? She felt as though her life had started to crumble.

***

Teal was a few minutes late to lunch because she had to stay behind after class to ask the history teacher, Miss Lynne, about the grade on her project about Alexander Graham Bell. She believed she should have received a better mark. Not the 75 she had been given. Teal felt she deserved at least an 80, if not higher.

Now, to back up her case, Teal had to type a ten-point bulletin on why she felt she should get a higher grade.

This was the way Miss Lynne always did it. She listened to a student's reasoning but then, to make it official for consideration, they had to write it out and hand it in.

Luckily, Teal already had a few points in mind. Tonight she would type them up and submit the bulletin tomorrow. Miss Lynne would have to boost her mark to at least the 80. She hoped.

Outside the caf, Teal spotted Olive as she sat at their usual table. There was food on her plate but Olive wasn't actually eating it. She was pushing the food around with her fork. Two more steps and Teal would have been in the cafeteria. Would. Have. Been.

Brad stepped right in front of her and blocked her path.

Teal couldn't take another step. She stood her ground and glared at him.

This seemed eerily familiar. Teal sensed another message about to unfold. What did he want now?

"You have to talk to Olive. Tell her to give me another chance. I don't really like Trina. It's just… You know. She pays for everything and I like that. But I want to be with Olive."

Teal raised her eyebrows. He thought it was okay to break her friend's heart? Cheat with another girl? Would it have been worse if it had been with a guy instead? And because the other chick had more money? Brad was way more of an ass than she'd originally thought.

"*NO.*" Teal replied loudly enough for everyone within earshot to hear.

It worked. She wanted people to hear what was going on. No way was she going to let him get away with this.

But Brad remained in place.

Maybe it was because Teal was pissed off, but without thinking, she dropped her bag to the floor and in one swift move, she used both hands, slammed them against his chest and pushed as hard as she could.

"*NO MEANS NO!*"

Suddenly, Teal felt confident and in control.

Brad was caught off guard. He lost his balance, slipped and hit the floor like a sack of potatoes.

Teal watched him.

The other students started to gather around. This was high-school entertainment at its finest.

Teal wasn't able to force herself to move. She waited. Surely Principal Marcus would arrive any moment to drag her off to his office. He would probably call the police as well. There was a good chance she would be charged with assault and hauled off in handcuffs.

Getting arrested would definitely gain Teal bragging rights. Her mother would be furious with her though. Maybe she should ask the principal to call her father instead. Teal knew she was in trouble but she could still feel the adrenaline as it rushed through her veins. At the moment, she didn't care.

Teal didn't move. Anyone else with common sense would have walked off to the sidelines to see the rest of the adventure unfold. Perhaps even pretend not to be involved. But not Teal.

Suddenly, Olive was beside Teal. Olive stared down at Brad. Teal was proud that he was still on the floor.

He seemed to be nursing his right leg. Brad hadn't moved even as Olive started to close in on him.

"I don't want anything to do with you ever again. Stay away from me and stay away from Teal. For good!"

With her teeth clenched, Olive threw her school bag over her shoulder and walked right out of the building and off school property.

Teal ran to catch up with her and together they walked to the coffee shop a couple blocks away where they sat and sipped on coffee for the rest of the lunch hour.

They talked about the good times they had growing up, that their friendship meant a lot to them and there was no way either one of them would ever let some boy come between them again. That was now part of The Code.

8

SATURDAY MORNING TEAL WENT to her father's. She had been looking forward to spending time with him. She wanted to let him know that things were now better between her and Olive. Teal didn't share everything with her parents. They didn't need to know the gritty details of her life. It was hard enough dealing with everything and everyone, let alone having her parents meddling in her personal life. Her parent's didn't believe in The Code and thought it was rubbish. But occasionally, Teal threw them a bone.

Teal especially had not wanted to hear another story from either of her parents that began with "When I was your age…" Teal guessed that parents believed that by sharing their own personal experiences it would somehow make everything magically better. This was not true. In fact, the stories usually made Teal feel worse.

Again, Teal didn't want to use her key at her father's.

She knocked and couldn't help but drop her jaw when Tonya answered the door. Worse yet, she kissed both of Teal's cheeks and hugged her like they were long-lost sisters. What the hell was this chick on? They were not cuddly best friends. This was not happening. Damn it. Teal had only met her once. That was it. Tonya was trying way too hard to win her over. It was backfiring for sure. What a mess.

"Is Dad here?"

"Yeah. He's in the bedroom changing Toby."

Wait. What? Toby was a kid? No. This had to be a mistake. Or maybe it was a bad prank.

Teal put one foot in front of the other cautiously and made her way to her father's bedroom. As soon as she entered, she stopped in her tracks.

On the bed was a half-naked little boy and her father was trying to change his diaper. Her father turned and looked up at Teal and smiled. This confirmed that both her father and Tonya were on drugs and had conspired with each other.

"I'll be with you in just a minute, Teal."

This was good because Teal needed time to figure out just what the hell was going on. Who was this kid? Teal knew her father believed all kids were brats. Well, all kids except Teal, of course.

Her father finished diaper duty and as soon as the kid had his pants back on, he hopped off the bed and made a run for it. "Mommy, Mommy, Mommy!"

Teal raised her eyebrows. Mommy? What was going on? Seriously?

"I want you to officially meet Toby. Tonya's son. He

just turned three." Her dad smiled.

And all this time Teal had thought Toby was a cat. Although she guessed this did explain why Tonya hadn't wanted a play date with her dog, Piper. First, she had to deal with the whole situation with Tonya and now she found out she had a kid? Tonya had a snotty, diaper-wearing son? This was too much for Teal.

Why did things never stay the same? Another mess. Teal wished she could use some sort of code to deal with all of this bullshit.

The kid was the last straw!

Her father was entitled to his life with someone after her mother. This, Teal could understand. But to not tell her he was seeing someone, and then invite Tonya over was not cool. Teal hadn't even started on the whole Toby situation.

Her father had tried to convince Toby to go see Teal, but the kid was more interested in the dump truck he was rolling back and forth on the living room floor.

Tonya just stood there smiling at Teal. Seriously? Was she being filmed for a hot new prank show?

"I'm leaving." Teal stated as she grabbed her backpack and stomped to the door. She heard her father call out to Tonya that he would be back in a minute.

"What's your problem, Teal?" He questioned as she stepped into the lobby.

Her dad was seriously asking this question? Did he think Teal would just be happy-go-lucky with everything?

It was not going to happen. Teal stared at him. It was obvious the man standing before her was not her real dad. Maybe the real one had been abducted.

"I cannot believe you even have to ask me that." Teal gave him the dirtiest look she could muster without crying.

She didn't wait for an answer. She ran outside to the sidewalk and kept running. All the way back to her mom's apartment.

Teal unlocked the door.

Unfortunately for Teal, her mother was back from her horticulture class. Teal was not in the mood. Her mother stood up but didn't move. Good call on her part even though she sensed Teal was upset.

"Teal? Is everything okay with your dad?" To her credit, she did seem genuinely concerned.

Teal dropped her bag on the living room floor.

"No. He has a new family and doesn't need me anymore." Teal hadn't given her time to reply. At this point what her mother said wouldn't matter. Teal needed time to be on her own to mull things over. This stuff took time. It was not going to magically fix itself.

***

Teal spent the rest of the day in her room. She listened to music, wrote in her journal and played online games. She thought about her life without her father in it. At this point, that thought hadn't seemed so bad. She would still have her mom and Olive.

Her father called her three times. He sent a text message saying he needed to talk to her as soon as possible.

Fat chance on that. Teal had no plans to speak to him anytime soon.

Teal decided to call Olive about the situation with her dad. Olive loved her parents. In fact, most of the time when Teal was in trouble, Olive would take their side and Teal hated it. Clearly, Olive needed to brush up on The Code for friendship. But this time, it seemed Teal did, in fact, have the right to be upset. Teal gave Olive all the gritty details and Olive laughed about the part where Teal had thought Toby was a cat.

As they hung up the phone, Teal smiled. She felt better. Wrongly assuming that Toby was a cat was funny. Just not at the time.

9

THE FOLLOWING SATURDAY, instead of going to her father's, Teal decided to blow off some steam and made plans to go over to Olive's for a girl's night. They planned to watch scary movies, paint their nails and gossip about Trina who had now left Brad. They would do whatever they wanted.

As Teal walked into the living room and grabbed a can of pop before heading out, her mother came up and wrapped her arms around her.

"Teal, you can't avoid your dad forever. I know that how he went about things was wrong. He should have talked to you first and taken things one step at a time. But as usual, he jumped into things right away and thought only of himself. You know your father. It's the way he is sometimes." She waited for Teal to say something.

Teal wondered why her mother was taking his side. Damn it, she needed to read The Parent Code.

"I know, Mom, I just need time." Teal wasn't sure what else she wanted her to say.

Over the last week, her father had called her three times every day and had sent text messages letting her know he loved her and hoped to hear from her soon.

Teal patted Piper on the head before she left for Olive's.

***

When Teal arrived, Olive showed her a text she'd received from Trina. In the text, Trina had apologized for the whole situation with Brad. Trina wanted to meet up with Olive to talk things through.

Wow! Tonight was going to be an adventure for sure. Someone besides Teal had a mess to clean up. Teal felt better just knowing she wasn't the only one dealing with crap.

They ordered in a large pizza and sat on Olive's bed.

As they waited for the food to arrive, they flipped through magazines. Olive was always on the lookout for the hottest guys to cut out and hang in her locker at school. Teal preferred to look for big words that stood out and other pictures she liked, except for Shemar. Shemar could go in her locker. As Teal cut out different items from the magazine, she pasted them into her journal. Art calmed Teal and helped her focus. On the plus side, she'd been especially creative over the last couple of weeks.

As they devoured an entire pizza between the two of them, Olive decided she wasn't ready to deal with boys. She had also made the decision to get together and talk to Trina. There was just no way Brad was going to win this round. Teal agreed with the part about Olive meeting up with Trina.

The part about Olive not being ready to deal with boys was also true. Although Olive said it all the time, the truth was she was boy crazy. Teal knew her friend. By next week Olive would have a crush on some new boy and would be spending her time chasing him down. Teal hoped the next guy wouldn't attend their school or at least not be in any of Teal's classes. Olive could deal with drama in the guy department on her own. Teal had enough on her plate as it was. Life was complicated enough without adding guys to the mix.

After they ate, Teal checked her cell. There was another text message from her father. It was another one of his "I love you" texts. Teal stared at it.

Olive asked if it was her dad again.

Teal nodded.

Olive didn't respond, but rolled her eyes. This was her way of telling Teal to get over it. It was easy for Olive, it wasn't her father.

Teal was tired of the situation though. She decided to pick up her cell and sent the same words back to him.

He responded right away with a smiley face. A second later, he sent another text. He wanted to get together for coffee the next afternoon.

Teal replied sure, as long as he came by himself.

He promised it would just be the two of them.

Teal breathed a sigh of relief. Just them, no Tonya, no Toby and no diapers for her dad to change. This worked for her.

Now Dad just had to keep his word.

***

The next morning when Teal arrived home, there was a small package on her bed. It was heavy. She shook it, but it didn't make a sound. Her mother wasn't home to ask but she was sure it was not a gift from her. When her mother bought her something, she always left it on the kitchen table. She was sure it wasn't from her father, either. What was it and who had sent it? There was only one way to find out.

Slowly, Teal tore open the teacup-printed wrapping paper, managing to save a piece of it. The paper was pretty.

Inside was a journal. It was also printed with antique cups and saucers. She opened up the cover to check and see what the pages felt like. They were lined and smooth. On the left, inside cover was a handwritten message.

Teal,

Sometimes it helps to write things out, and over time, the answers will appear as though they have been waiting to be revealed by you this entire time. I was a teenager once, too.

Your friend,

Miss Tate

Miss Tate? *Why?* Better yet, how had she known that a journal was something Teal would actually like. She sat on her bed and held the journal close to her. The gift was precious. Never had she ever thought she would consider Miss Tate as anything other than the grumpy woman who lived next door. Things had changed between them since the day Teal took tea at Miss Tate's place (and used up a box of tissues) after a meltdown. Teal and Miss Tate were now friends.

Miss Tate now waved a small hello when Teal ran into her in hallway. Now she had given her a journal. Miss Tate had taken the time to pick it out and Teal appreciated it. Every time she saw tea cups from now on, she would think of Miss Tate who had taken the time to listen to her and who had also been a teenager once.

Suddenly, Teal felt silly. She had let herself get all sentimental over something like this. It was a strange feeling knowing that someone cared about her. Of course, there was her mom and her dad but it was their job to care. Teal had always figured that was part of The Parent Code.

Teal placed the journal down. She took out her art supplies and over the next hour, she made a special card for Miss Tate. It had been thoughtful to invite her in and even more so to give her this journal. Teal had to let her know she got it and how much she appreciated it.

After she finished making the card, she walked out into the hallway and slipped it under Miss Tate's door. She hoped Miss Tate would find it first thing in the morning when she headed out for her daily walk.

10

Teal felt good after dropping off the card to Miss Tate so she decided to head over to Starbucks. She had twenty minutes before her father was to show up. She wanted a few minutes to breathe and brace herself just in case Tonya showed up with him. Teal had already decided that if Tonya was with him, it would make him a liar. If her father respected and cared for her, he would come alone as he'd promised. She crossed her fingers and hoped he would arrive soon. Teal was at the coffee shop. The rest was up to him.

Ten minutes later, Teal saw her father come in. She held her breath for nearly a whole minute. She expected Toby to run through the coffee shop or Tonya to be right behind him where she wasn't able to see her right away. Teal was prepared to make a run for it.

He spotted her quickly and walked over to the table. Even after he was seated, Teal kept looking at the door. She was sure Tonya would be joining them at any moment.

"She's not here, Teal. She isn't coming. I told you it would be just us." Her dad glanced at the door and looked at Teal with raised eyebrows.

Teal rolled her eyes. She didn't care. She waited for him to start talking. After all, he was the one who'd suggested they meet up. Not to mention he was the one who had some explaining to do, not her.

Finally, in a loving voice, he started. "I am sorry, Teal. I should have told you about Tonya."

Teal didn't reply right away. It was hard, but her father needed to know that she was serious about the whole Tonya and Toby situation. She hoped he had a lot more to say. So far, he had definitely not said enough. But it was a good start.

"I've been seeing Tonya for a couple of months and I really wanted you to meet her. I should have given you a heads-up and arranged for Tonya to meet you on neutral ground. Like all of us going out for supper or something instead of just having her show up at my place. I honestly thought you would be excited about having Toby around. You love kids."

He waited for her to say something.

Teal could tell he was nervous because he kept tapping his right finger on his right leg. He always did that when he was stressed. Especially when he had unexpected news to drop. He had a habit of getting himself into jams just like this one. Her mother couldn't stand it. It had been one of the stupid things they'd fought about constantly.

"Dad, I thought Toby was a cat." Teal breathed in deeply.

"A cat?" She could tell he was trying to stifle laughter.

Teal couldn't help herself. She burst out laughing. It was funny now but at the time, it had been anything but.

"What made you think Toby was a cat?"

"Well… Tonya and I were talking and she mentioned Toby. She said he was the same age as Piper was so I just thought she meant Toby was a cat or maybe even a dog. Not for one second did I think she meant Toby was her son."

"That's funny," said her dad. "It is."

Teal continued to sip her tea. It wasn't nearly as good as Miss Tate's. The whole situation was uncomfortable. She was glad they were having this conversation out in public.

Her dad remained silent.

Teal continued on with her tea, reminding herself that at any time she could get up and walk out, and there was nothing her dad could do about it. She liked this feeling of power. Probably a little too much.

"All right, Teal. Can we start over again? With Tonya?"

Teal was baffled. How could they possibly start over? Did he want her to pretend like Tonya didn't exist? She asked what in the world he was talking about. It had seemed they'd been making progress. The last thing she wanted to do was throw it away.

"Well. We could meet up with Tonya—just Tonya—and have supper together somewhere. You can pick the place. And we'll take it from there. That way, Tonya won't be in your personal space. And if you don't want to stay for dessert, I'll understand and I'll respect your decision. But you have to sit with us for at least half an hour to give Tonya a chance. I… I care about her."

Her dad sounded sincere. He was even willing to spring for dinner out. This wasn't like him at all. He was always saying things were overpriced and he had better things to spend his money on. This could be serious after all.

Teal nodded. At least this time, he was keeping her in the loop. She decided now was a good time to leave.

***

She took her time walking home. She wanted to think. It didn't look like Tonya would be leaving any time soon. She had to accept the situation for what it was. At least for now. She would have to meet up with Tonya and get to know her. Who knew, maybe once she got to know Toby, he wouldn't be so bad. How much trouble can a three-year-old be?

***

Teal arrived home and immediately spotted a card on her bed, with her name on it. She picked it up and opened it.

It was a thank-you card from Miss Tate. This made her smile. She guessed the two of them would be keeping in touch. This was a good thing.

She grabbed Piper from the living room and curled up with him on the bed. She had some quiet time to herself. Things were starting to work themselves out.

She scratched Piper behind his ear. "You know, Piper, things are good with Olive. Things with Dad are looking hopeful. Miss Tate and I are now friends. Even Mom hasn't labeled me rude in over a week and that might be some kind of a record." She picked her dog up and rubbed noses with him. "Lately, Mom has seemed distracted, though. I don't know what that means but as long as *she* doesn't bring a straggler home, I just might be able to manage."

Things sometimes moved too fast for Teal and this made her feel as though she didn't have time to breathe. Not to mention all the effort it took trying to keep everyone else happy.

It wasn't long before her mother arrived home and they sat down to one of her favorite meals: baked ratatouille. Her mother even surprised Teal with cheesecake for dessert. Chocolate cheesecake was Teal's absolute favorite sweet. She enjoyed the meal as they made small talk.

She was actually expecting her mother to spring some sort of news she would not be happy about. But no. Her mother didn't do it. No. No new drama. She asked Teal how the coffee date went with her dad had gone and wanted to know if Teal would be spending the night at his place this coming weekend.

Teal let her know she'd be meeting up with him for supper, but other than that... Really, it all depended on how things went down at supper.

11

Teal and her father exchanged texts as they made plans for supper out with Tonya. It was up to Teal to pick the place and she had decided on Red Lobster. She figured she might as well get what she could out of the deal. They were now on the same page. It was a start. Teal was making an effort, and hopefully, her father would notice.

With supper plans made, Teal and Piper cuddled up on the couch to watch a new episode of *Criminal Minds*. No journaling, no homework, no texting. Just time with Piper and Shemar. It felt nice. Olive had sent her a text to update Teal on the new guy. His name was Tank. Teal didn't bother to send a reply. Olive's dramatic lifestyle could waste an entire evening. Teal would get more details on him later. Not that she needed any. She was sure Olive's new adventure would be short lived.

***

Teal arrived at Red Lobster for five o'clock, as they had agreed. Her dad was already there waiting. They grabbed a booth and waited for Tonya to show up. In Teal's books, her dad scored extra points by not showing up with Tonya holding onto his arm. She was grateful for this small favor. He smiled at Teal as they snacked on delicious cheese biscuits and sipped on cold soft drinks while they waited for Tonya.

Tonya arrived fifteen minutes later. She greeted her dad with a kiss on each cheek. She flashed Teal a smile and apologized for being late. The babysitter was late showing up to watch Toby because she had missed a bus.

This was good. Tonya already had a babysitter. Teal didn't want her thinking that just because she was old enough and didn't have any siblings of her own, she would be willing to watch Toby whenever Tonya wanted her to. There was no way she would be left with Toby on her own anytime in the near future.

Then Teal reminded herself to take things one day at a time. There wasn't any point in getting herself all worked up for something that may or may not happen. They'd only been together for a few months.

For supper, Teal ordered the shrimp linguini. Tonya and her dad each ordered a steak. Teal raised her eyebrows in surprise. She'd figured Tonya would order a salad or something equally healthy. Maybe Tonya wasn't so bad after all. Maybe this could work. Maybe.

Tonya liked scrapbooking. She talked a lot about a "cute store" that had recently opened in the newest local mall. It was called Crafts & Things. Teal remembered her mom mentioning that the store would be opening soon. It did sound awesome. It seemed like there might be many interesting things Teal could decorate her journals with. Tonya suggested they check out the store together sometime.

"Sure," Teal replied tentatively.

The craft store was not a whole lot to go on but it was a start. Teal was working on the promise she had made to her dad.

Supper was delicious. A half hour had come and gone. Teal could now leave if she wanted to. That had been the deal. But Teal decided to share a piece of Black Forest cake with her dad. Tonya ordered a coffee.

Teal was glad they got to share the cake. For some reason, it brought back good memories of the old days when her parents were still together. Teal knew there was no way they would be getting back together but these little moments brought her a sense of comfort. She wished she could enjoy more times like this. Teal tried to block out everything else in her mind and focus on how happy she felt at this particular moment. She always spent too much time stressing and worrying about everything. Therefore, when the good moments did arrive, she sometimes forgot to enjoy them.

As Teal licked the delicious remains of the cake from the fork, Tonya asked if she wanted to stop off at the mall and check out the store after they were finished eating.

Teal paused. This was somewhat soon. She figured she would have had time to mentally prepare for her adventure. She wasn't sure what to say. Clearly, Tonya was putting in the effort. What if Teal said no and Tonya was insulted? What if things got worse between them? It was time for Teal to play her maturity card.

"Sure. Sounds great."

Tonya and her dad looked at each other and smiled.

Another small step. They would see how this adventure turned out.

***

The store was impressive. There was so much to look at, Teal could have spent hours browsing.

Tonya showed her some things she had tried and liked to use. She was currently working on a scrapbook for her aunt.

There were so many different types of stamps, craft paper and gel pens. The store apparently had everything, but Teal hadn't even seen the most-impressive stuff yet. Was Tonya saving the best for last?

Half an hour after entering the store, Tonya told Teal to turn around. Teal turned and inhaled deeply.

Before her stood an entire wall dedicated to different types of journals. There were too many to even count. Teal rifled through a few. They were all different shapes and sizes.

Tonya told Teal she could pick out two journals and one gel pen to go with each journal. This was completely unexpected but she immediately started narrowing down her choices. There was a good chance Tonya was just trying to buy her off. At least she was making an effort so Teal had to put in the effort, too.

It was another half hour before Teal had finally picked the two journals she wanted. One was black and white with a checkered pattern. The other was white with a vintage map in black on it. She also picked out a purple and a pink gel pen to go with her journals. This would keep her busy for a bit.

So far, so good.

While at the cash, Tonya's cell phone rang. Tonya checked her message. It was a text from her sitter. Toby was sick. He was sick and he wanted his mommy.

At this news, Teal figured Tonya would just walk out and leave to be with Toby.

But Tonya didn't. She stayed and paid for Teal's stuff.

Two more bonus points for Tonya. Tonya hadn't even rushed her.

As they left the mall, Tonya said she had to go but had enjoyed the evening and hoped to see Teal again soon.

"Same here," Teal replied. The funny thing was, she honestly meant it. This was only a start, but it was a good one.

Tonya left to go back home to take care of Toby.

Teal and her father decided to go back to his place and Teal sent a text letting her mother know she had decided to spend the weekend at her dad's.

Her mom replied back with a smiley face.

12

THE NEXT MORNING, Teal and her father made their usual chocolate-chip pancakes together. Her father also made mint hot chocolate to go with them and added the mini-marshmallows.

Her dad was truly awesome.

They sat in their pajamas for two hours as they made breakfast, ate together and chatted. It had felt just like old times.

Later on in the afternoon, they decided to go see the latest action movie and after the show, he drove her back to her mom's.

Before he left, he told Teal he hoped to see her again soon.

She replied with "Ditto."

***

For once it seemed like everyone was happy, including

Teal. She and her father were on the same page. She was still best friends with Olive. The confusing dreams had vanished. Teal was good friends with Miss Tate. Brad was out of the picture. Things with her mom were good.

Note to self: Life is good. Enjoy the special moments, the bad ones will eventually pass. Life is better with a best friend, a dog, and chocolate cheesecake.

Not Again

13

Teal's birthday was coming up. She wanted to make sure it would be a birthday not to forget. It had to be memorable. Certain birthday numbers counted more than others did. For example, sixteen, eighteen, nineteen and twenty would be the big ones. Things were different when you were sixteen. At eighteen you were officially an adult. At nineteen you didn't need to pay someone else to go to the liquor store and buy the alcohol for you. And at twenty, your teen years were over and you were supposed to start building a life of your own. This year she would be sixteen, a milestone.

Teal reminded herself there would be plenty of time when she got home later to think and figure out stuff for her birthday. For now, she needed to focus on her visit with her friendly neighbor, Miss Tate.

She sat down on Miss Tate's couch and waited for their ritual to start: having tea and discussing their lives.

Mostly hers, but every so often Miss Tate chimed in with something of her own. Over the last few months, they had fallen into a bit of a routine, which included Teal's stopping by for tea after supper on Sundays. She visited almost every weekend. The visit usually lasted an hour and a half, which seemed just the right amount of time. Staying for an hour would seem rushed, and staying over two hours was simply too much for both of them.

Miss Tate handed her a cup of tea. How Teal loved Miss Tate's tea! She didn't know what her secret was, but her tea was the best. Teal asked her why it tasted so good. Miss Tate nodded and politely said it would remain secret. However, she had once told her that when something was made with love it naturally tasted a whole lot better. Maybe that was really the answer. Teal once tried going into the kitchen while Miss Tate was making the tea. Miss Tate's eyes had opened wide and she actually shooed her out! She would never attempt something as silly as that again.

"So your sweet sixteen birthday is in a couple of weeks. Do you have any plans yet?" Miss Tate asked.

Of course she had plans. She was going to be sixteen years old, practically an adult. Okay, not really, but close. She smiled. It was just a matter of time before she lived on her own. Of course she would have a fabulous job and the other things she wanted. That's what being an adult was about, getting to do what you want, when you wanted. There would be responsibilities but just the freedom itself would far outweigh the consequences.

She looked around the apartment once again. Something had changed since the last time she had visited but she could not put a finger on it. Miss Tate saw her looking and just smiled. Whatever it was, she sure was not going to tell.

"I am planning on going out with Olive and a few others to the spring fair in the evening. We want to ride the merry-go-round, Ferris wheel and play games. I'm not a hundred percent sure what we're going to do during the day yet. I'm sure we'll find something. It doesn't really matter as long as I spend time with my friends."

"Sounds like a good day. Just make sure you don't get into any trouble. You know how easily that can happen nowadays. I once heard someone say 'just thirty seconds of something, good or bad, can change your life forever'." Miss Tate's eyes got large again. She was such an interesting lady. Teal never really could predict what she would say next.

Teal nodded in agreement. *Yes, we reckless teenagers do not know what we are doing anymore. It seems as though our parents and other authority figures are always surprised to see we manage to get dressed by ourselves each morning. Really, it was a miracle. What was our country coming to?*

As she stood to leave, it finally hit her. She knew what the difference was in Miss Tate's apartment. It was the frogs. She seemed to be collecting frogs. A couple dozen of them were lined up along the bookcase and the TV stand.

"What's with the frogs? Do they remind you of someone?"

"Oh, well, no. I enjoy checking out the little second-hand stores in the market when the weather is nice. I need to get exercise. Plus it's kind of fun." She smiled.

It was good to hear that she was getting out more. Lately she seemed in a better mood. Teal liked to think it was because of all the extra attention she received from her stopping in regularly for tea and all.

"There is no rush or anything, but I was wondering if you could mail a letter to my cousin Dottie for me? While you are out walking Piper in the next couple of days would be fine. If you don't mind."

"No problem." She took the letter from Miss Tate.

"Well thanks for coming, Teal. It was great seeing you again."

"Thanks."

14

Teal walked into her apartment.

"How's Miss Tate?" Her mother inquired.

"Good. Apparently she has a new hobby."

Her mother raised her eyebrows. Probably trying to decide if Teal was being sarcastic or not. Good call.

"I'm serious. She has started collecting frogs. Yep, frogs. Not sure why. But she says she enjoys hunting them down or something like that at the second-hand stores." She grabbed a can of Coke from the fridge.

"At least she is getting out—she must be in her seventies or eighties by now."

Teal shrugged. She honestly had no idea. "Oh, the stuff I have to look forward to down the road."

Her mother laughed as Teal headed toward her room.

Perhaps she thought she was trying to be funny but really, that's what she was thinking.

***

Teal checked her phone. Ugh. There still wasn't a single message from Olive. Did she not know she was sitting here waiting to find out? Jay had to pull through for us. Not that he owed us anything. Still, it wasn't as if we were expecting him to do it for free or anything. Besides, it was for her birthday. Jay really sounded like someone they could count on. Then again, they had no idea what he was like. They'd heard his name from a friend of a friend. That meant it had to be legit. If a friend vouched for someone, it usually meant they could be trusted.

She decided to take Piper out for a walk. As she stared at the phone, she realized it wasn't going to make Olive get back to her any faster. At least there was more room to pace around outside.

A couple blocks later she ran into Jackson and his mother. He held a package from Hopper's bakery.

"Hey, Jackson. Hey, Em." She smiled. "Are you still able to come to the fair with us on my birthday?"

"I wouldn't miss it. Of course I will be there." Jackson smiled back.

"Just make sure you kids stay out of trouble. You know how it can be these days. Some parents just let their kids run wild and it doesn't take much. I know you guys are good, but you have to watch out for some of the others." Em laughed but seemed genuine. That was sweet of her. She seemed to have a lot in common with Teal's own mother.

***

Once back at home Teal gave Piper a dog treat and checked her messages. Nothing from Olive. Teal decided to send another message anyway. Worse case, Olive would be frustrated but Teal was willing to risk it today.

She messaged Olive:

> Do we have a plan B?
>
> We don't need a plan B!

At least she was confident. That was a good sign. She would let it go for now. Her birthday was still a few weeks away. There wasn't any point in getting herself worked up. A lot can happen between now and then. Hopefully, this Jay person would let them know what the deal was.

She made her way back to the kitchen and grabbed a couple of cookies to munch on while she wrote in her journal. On the way back, she noticed her mother at the computer. Usually, after eight in the evening, she didn't watch TV, go on the computer, or even check her phone for messages. She just read and relaxed. As she walked by, her mother blocked the screen. A red flag that something was up for sure.

"Um, what are you doing, Mom?" It was obvious she did not want her to see what she was up to.

"Nothing. Um, just online shopping." She tapped her foot, a clear indication she was lying.

Teal decided it would be a waste of time to say anything else for the moment. However, she was curious as to what her mother had been working on. Ah, maybe she was setting up some sort of dating profile. One of the ones Teal had heard about was Plenty of Fish. She shivered. Gross. Of course her mother had every right to move on with her life. Her father had. Her mother was single. She deserved to be happy. Still, as she pictured her parents dating at any age, it didn't seem cool.

She tried to put it out of her mind. It was best if she did not think about her mother bringing someone around. It might never happen, or it could happen the next week for all she knew. There wasn't any point in worrying about it. Now if she came home and there was some strange man in the house, then they would need to have a talk. Teal's mother had been aware of how she had been feeling and dealt with the episode of once upon a time when she had gone over to her father's to spend the weekend and had walked in to see a strange woman sitting on the couch. Things had not started great. In time, things had worked themselves out. He was still with the girl from the couch, Tonya.

Teal decided to write in her journal before hopping in for a quick shower. She turned the journal to the page she was currently working on. She was nearly finished this journal, just a few dozen pages left. Writing helped when she felt stressed. She worried about her party, her mother using dating websites, and if Quinn would even show up to her birthday. Nothing big, just a gathering at Olive's house before they went to the fair. She really wanted him to come to her birthday but didn't want anyone to know just how much. Maybe Quinn didn't even like her. He had smiled at her and stuff, but he seemed to do that with all the girls so maybe he was just being polite. Maybe that was just his character. How could she find out if he liked her without letting him know that she liked him? It was too complicated. How did Olive do it? The more she thought about Quinn, well, maybe it wouldn't be such a good idea to get Olive to help her. Maybe she would think about it more in the shower.

As she dried herself off, she realized she didn't have a choice. Either she could try to figure things out with Quinn on her own, with absolutely no experience, or she could involve Olive and maybe have a slim shot. Slim was definitely better than nothing. But she needed a plan and then had to get Olive on board with said plan.

15

TEAL'S FATHER SENT A TEXT MESSAGE. He wanted to have a talk. Whenever he said something like that, it was always important. He did mention it would just be the two of them. They would have a quiet supper somewhere. This was not a regular thing. In fact, the more she thought about it, the last time it had been just she and her father, it was before he had started dating Tonya. Maybe things with him and Tonya hadn't worked out. Hmm, she had to think about it. She wasn't sure how she felt. Teal knew her parents were not getting back together. Tonya was a decent person. No one could compare to her mother, but Tonya had been okay. Teal had tried hard *not* to like her, but they ended up getting along. She felt as though Tonya respected her and not once had Tonya ever tried to step in and play the "I am your stepmother" card. Definitely a good sign. Her father seemed happy. He deserved to be. He was only in his late forties and had another lifetime ahead of him. She hoped things between her father and Tonya were still good because if they weren't, then eventually down the road, there would be someone else new. The last thing she wanted to do was to start from scratch again.

And then there was Toby. He was growing on her. Any time he saw her, he came running, yelling "Tee" while he clapped his hands. Of course she couldn't help but roll her eyes when it happened but deep down it touched her heart. It made her feel wanted when sometimes she felt just the opposite. Toby had been so adorable at Christmas, opening up presents with such excitement. She had spent Christmas Eve at her father's with all of them. They had decorated the tree together. The two of them had built a gingerbread house which ended up being the worst she had ever seen in her life. At the same time, she'd had so much fun. It was something she wouldn't forget any time soon. It would be nice if it became a yearly tradition.

Finally, her father arrived. He looked around the restaurant for a moment before he saw Teal and walked toward her. He had allowed her to pick the place and she had decided on her favorite pasta place, Robbie's.

"Hey, Teal," he said as he hugged her.

"Good to see you, Dad." And she meant it. It was nice just to be with him one-on-one for a bit. Well, that was if everything was okay. She was kind of worried.

"What do you say we order our food and then chat. If that's okay with you?"

"Yes, Dad. I already asked for an order of garlic bread with cheese."

He nodded. "Of course I am going to have the Robbie's Spaghetti Special."

"Lasagna for me." She didn't need to open the menu. Robbie's lasagna was one of her favorites. Sometimes sticking to the same things brought comfort. It was too early to tell if she would need comfort in this particular case but better to be prepared.

As the garlic bread arrived, her father wanted to get down to business.

"So things are going well with Tonya. I'm curious to know how you're feeling about her now. She's been around for a while and you have spent a lot of time with her and Toby. You spent Christmas with us." Here, her father paused as if unsure if he should keep going or just stop there.

Teal let out a huge breath that she hadn't realized she'd been holding.

She waited a moment and when he didn't continue, she decided he was probably waiting for her to say something.

"I think things are going really well."

She paused and picked up another piece of garlic bread before she continued.

"Um, and yeah. Christmas was pretty cool with her and Toby. I think she's good for you, Dad." She looked down at her plate.

She felt her father staring at her. Maybe this was not what he'd expected her to say.

"Really, Teal? Is that really how you feel? You aren't just saying that because it's something you think I want to hear?" His eyes widened.

"Honest, Dad. I wouldn't lie about something like this. I know how much she means to you and I want you to be happy. I know Tonya and I didn't hit it off too well when I found her sitting on my couch, but we have come a long way. Plus. Toby can be fun sometimes, and I know you are really happy."

This time she looked directly at her father.

Neither of them said a word for nearly a full minute.

"I really care for Tonya and Toby," he said. "In fact, I was wondering what you would think if I asked her to marry me?" Her father automatically started tapping his foot.

Her father only tapped his foot when he was nervous. Her mother tapped hers when she was lying. Sometimes parents think they are so clever. Teal had this all figured out years ago but had never said anything. It was an advantage, a small one, but still.

"When are you thinking about getting married? Like right away?" This was interesting.

"No, I'll ask her and if she says yes, we'll talk about it and make sure you're comfortable with the time frame as well. I would like to involve you as much as possible. I was thinking anywhere from six months to two years from now. Of course, that's only my thoughts—I still have to talk it over with Tonya. I may have to put on the brakes with the whole topic of marriage though. I might be getting ahead of myself here. Let's wait and see if she says yes first."

"Well, if she says no, then she is definitely not the one for you, Dad!" Teal smiled.

"Glad you are on board with it. It really does mean a

lot to me, Teal. One last thing I want to ask your opinion on." Her father paused.

She waited. She knew there had to be a catch or something. Why had she let her guard down in the first place? Of course, several things in a row could not just magically go her way. She decided to keep quiet and wait for him to continue.

"Well, you know how Tonya and Toby have been spending more time at my place slowly moving in. Well, uh… I would like to adopt Toby. It's a bit of a process but I would like to start the paperwork soon so… Yeah…"

Teal definitely had something to say now. The look in her father's eyes said he needed her to say something. Adopting Toby was just as big as the wedding, if not bigger. If the marriage didn't work out, her father and Tonya would get a divorce but what about Toby? Her father wouldn't be able to divorce the kid. Right?

"I have a few questions first, if that's okay?" She didn't wait for a reply. She continued, needing to get it all out fast because she was embarrassed.

"Where is Toby's dad? Why doesn't he want him and let's say you adopt Toby and then things don't work out with Tonya? I mean I'm sure they will, but in case they don't, what happens to Toby?" She held her breath and waited.

"Toby's dad is in jail."

"What? No way! What did he do? Won't he want Toby back when he gets out?" It sounded like it could be a waste of time if her father went through all this trouble to adopt Toby and then have to give him up when his real father got out of jail. Pointless really.

"You don't need to know what he did. Just trust me when I say he will not be coming out for a very long time. Honestly, Teal, he has never actually seen his son. Tonya decided she wanted better for her and Toby. That's all I'm going to say on that piece. If I were to adopt Toby and things didn't work out between Tonya and me, I would still get to see him. That means you would still get to see him, too. He would come for visits and stuff because I legally would be his father." He gulped down a huge glass of water.

"I think it's great that we wouldn't have to give him back if things don't work out with Tonya. I mean of course they will, but good to know… just in case."

Over the top of her dessert menu, she saw her father smile. She, herself, couldn't believe her own ears. The little bugger was definitely growing on her. She might officially end up with a brother. Imagine that. She would be someone's older sibling. She just hoped nothing changed after they adopted Toby and her father and Tonya married. Like maybe, all of a sudden, they might expect her to babysit him all the time or something like that. She didn't mind doing it every so often, but she wasn't Toby's parents, they were.

16

As Teal closed the apartment door, she spotted her mother at the computer again. Only this time, her mother was slower at blocking the computer screen. If she had taken a fraction longer, Teal would have seen the screen. So close. Next time, she swore, she would creep into the apartment quickly and catch her in the act, to catch her mother in whatever she was up to. Teal was now even more determined to find out what was going on. She would figure it out later. Right now, she had to get ready to celebrate her sweet sixteenth birthday with a few of her friends.

***

Trina was the one who opened the door to Olive's house when Teal arrived. "Everyone's in the basement because there's more room. Olive's mom is already gone so that works out." Trina smiled and hugged her.

"Awesome. Was Olive able to get the goods?" Teal asked, holding her breath.

"Yep. And you are never going to believe who we got it from."

"My guesses are Jay, Sam or Connor. I've heard those names around the school more times than I can count."

"Nope. I'll let Olive tell you."

As soon as Teal reached the bottom step to the basement, Olive attacked in a big hug and cried out. "Happy Birthday!"

"Thanks." She already felt nervous. It seemed as though Olive had finished off a couple of drinks. Her breath reeked of alcohol. Usually, when Teal hung out with friends, it was Olive and one or two other people. Never really enough to call it a party. But tonight was going to be different. Already there were more people than she was generally comfortable with. Trina and Olive did not seem up to much. Vye and Lily sat on the couch, doing something on their phones, and two guys were playing a game of pool. One of them was Sam and the other one looked familiar but she couldn't remember his name.

Olive looked at the boys playing pool and back at Teal.

"You know him, right?" Olive nudged her.

"He looks familiar but I can't think of his name."

"It's Cody. Brad's older brother."

"Okay, what's he doing here? He isn't my friend or your friend." She crossed her arms in front of her chest. She wasn't happy. This was supposed to be her birthday.

"He's the one that got the alcohol for us. On the condition he could come. So I thought why not. The more the merrier right? Plus, really, what choice did we have? If I said no, then we wouldn't have anything to drink to celebrate your special night and what kind of party doesn't have alcohol? Especially a birthday party?" Olive made it seem like a great idea.

"Okay, I guess." Although she said it, Teal still was not sure. However, as Olive had said, what choice did they really have? Maybe she was just nervous because Quinn had not shown up yet. It was great to have a few different people, but the one she was interested in was Quinn.

Olive grabbed a bunch of shot glasses and placed them on the coffee table. Next, a large bottle of Crown Royal. She lined up a dozen glasses and filled them right to the brim. They were so full, Teal was sure they would spill over when Olive picked them up, but Olive didn't seem to care. It looked like all she wanted to do was get everybody at the table to start taking shots and therefore start the actual party.

A few minutes later, Quinn, Jackson, Mandy, Nirva and Zac showed up. Everyone seemed to be in a good mood. That was a good sign, Teal decided. Even better, now that Quinn had arrived.

By the third shot, Teal started feeling the alcohol. When Olive poured another round, she discreetly passed her shot glass to Nirva who was able to tolerate alcohol well. She and Zac were the only ones who did not continue taking shots. Although Zac had opened a beer and was drinking it on the side.

Once Olive realized that Teal was no longer taking shots, she grabbed a bottle of Caesar from the mini-fridge, popped it open and handed it to Teal. "It's your night. You have to try and keep up!" She bent over in a laughing fit.

"Thanks and cheers!" Teal replied. She just wanted to keep Olive out of her hair. If she had any more drinks, it would be because she chose to. Not because Olive said she should or because Olive was pushing the drinks on her. To keep the impression she was drinking, though, she made sure to have the bottle with her whenever and wherever she moved around the basement. It was easier that way. The last thing she needed was to end up in an argument with Olive. Especially on her own birthday.

When Zac challenged her to a game of sandbags, she won the first round. In the second, he beat her. And in the third, she won by a landslide. After watching the game, Nirva challenged her and to make things even more interesting, bet her twenty-five dollars that she couldn't beat her. Just one game, not the best of three.

Teal took a long swallow from her bottle. For some reason, she felt more intimidated to be playing against Nirva than when she had played against Zac. Was it because this was a bet? She told herself it didn't matter. It was just twenty-five dollars and she had the money on her. It wasn't as if this was serious or anything. They were all there to hang out, play games and have fun. They didn't want to arrive at the fair too early because they wanted to see all the lights and rides lit up. It would be more magical that way.

Just as they each grabbed their sandbags, everyone

stopped what they were doing in order to come and watch the two girls play against one another. Great, this made things even more nerve wracking for her. There was no way she could back out now, though. Everyone was watching. Not a good feeling, but she had to push it aside. It was her birthday. Maybe she would either win the game or they would take it easy on her if she lost because it was her birthday.

Ten minutes later, the game was tied, but Nirva had just taken her last turn so it was Teal's final turn. And now she knew exactly where the expression "it was so quiet you could hear a pin drop" came from. It was from moments like this. She tried to stay calm and reassured herself it wasn't worth it to get worked up. The score was tied. Even if she missed, they would still be tied and that would be fine by her. A tie meant a tie and not a loss.

She threw the bean bag.

Olive jumped on her.

What happened?

"Get off me. I can't breathe. What happened?" she yelled from a half sitting position on the carpet. It was obvious Olive had had too much drink.

"You won!" Olive clapped her hands and jumped up and down.

She couldn't help but smile. *Yes indeed. This was a good night.* She hoped things would stay this way.

17

The fair and night were going to be awesome. The sun was just setting and all the lights on the rides sparkled. Colored lights were everywhere. It made her smile as she tried to pretend this whole set-up was just for her birthday. One magical night. She definitely deserved it. She needed to let the worries slide and have fun. Unlike her, but then again, she was not the same kid anymore, she was maturing. Of course. She was sixteen years old.

As she looked around, she let out a small squeal. She couldn't wait to get started. So much to do. Where should we start? She wished moments like these could be stored in a jar to use later. She wanted the feeling to last. She was happy!

"What do you guys want to do first?" asked Mandy.

"I love the Tilt-A-Whirl. I'm game for that. Anyone with me?" Jackson chipped in.

Teal shook her head. That definitely was not a ride for her. It would make her sick on a good day and with the drinks she had consumed earlier, it would not be a good idea.

"I'll pass." Quinn looked directly at her.

She smiled. This was good.

"I want pink cotton candy. Who's with me?" Olive asked.

The group divided, with Jackson, Cody and Nirva heading to wait in the lineup for the Tilt-A-Whirl ride. Olive, Zac and Mandy made their way to the opposite end of the fair to grab some cotton candy. A couple minutes later, Quinn and Teal began walking around the fair looking at the games.

Teal's heart beat faster. Of course, she had hoped she would have the chance to be alone with Quinn. She wanted to make sure the move wasn't too noticeable. It seemed like fate. She couldn't believe that shortly after they arrived at the fair, an opportunity had presented itself. Perhaps, since it was her birthday, the odds were in her favor? That would be awesome, she thought. Maybe Quinn had set it up purposely.

She smiled.

"You have a beautiful smile." Quinn looked at her as they continued to walk.

Teal glanced in his direction. At his milk-chocolate eyes that she could have stared into forever.

"Thanks." She wasn't sure what else to say. She wanted to make sure she didn't say anything silly. It was always good manners to accept a compliment. *What happens now?* This might be her only chance with Quinn and she didn't want to blow it.

"You and Olive are pretty tight."

"Yeah, we've been friends nearly forever." This was good. He was asking questions. This meant he wanted to get to know her.

"Do you happen to know if Olive is currently seeing anyone? As in, does she have a boyfriend?" Quinn smiled at Teal. It looked to her like he was holding his breath as he waited for her reply.

She had to shake her head. What just happened? What had he just asked her? This was not happening. How could she have misread him? The compliment about her smile must have been a lie. He had said it just to butter her up so she would divulge information about Olive. She wanted to kick herself. She had let her guard down. It had all been a set-up. He had used her. No. Maybe she shouldn't jump to conclusions. She'd had enough experience in *that* department. It was best to let things take their course first.

"She isn't in a relationship. I know she was out on a few dates here and there but that's it. Nothing serious." Okay, she inhaled. She had given him an honest answer. They would move on and leave Olive out of it completely.

"Awesome. I wanted to be sure. Since you are best friends, could you please put in a good word for me? I want to ask her out on a date. I thought if you could say something to her, I might have a better shot than if I just ask on my own." Again, he looked excited and it had nothing to do with her. Not good at all.

She cringed. Now his motive was quite clear. It had

absolutely nothing to do with her. He had been nice just to get the information he wanted. No way she would tell him how she felt about him now. She was just glad she hadn't said anything else. What an embarrassment it would be. If she had told him, she would have had to transfer schools and things would have been more complicated. The last thing she needed. So far so good. She should be able to handle the damage control on her own.

She stood still, unsure of what the protocol was for situations like this. Not to mention the fact that she did not trust herself. The last thing she wanted to do was start crying or show Quinn that she was upset. She would not hand over her dignity that easily.

"I'm going to go see if Olive is still in line to go buy cotton candy. Maybe I can get it for her. On the other hand, if she already has some, I'll wait until she has her mouth full and then ask her out on a date. That way she has time to think about it while she finishes chewing. And remember to put in a good word for me if she asks!" Quinn winked and turned away.

Teal stood there still wondering what would happen next, although she was pretty sure she didn't want to know.

18

She found a washroom and stayed in a stall for a few minutes until most of her emotions were in check. Teal couldn't let this episode with Quinn ruin what was supposed to be her special evening. It sucked that it happened but what made it feel ten times worse was that it was her best friend that Quinn wanted.

Even in the security of the washroom, she still wasn't sure what to do. It was her party. Yes. But if she left because she was upset, she would never live it down. This was not how it was supposed to unfold. She was supposed to let Quinn know how she felt, then they would share a special kiss. In none of her previously worked out scenarios had she ever pictured Quinn asking her to match him up with her own best friend. How could she have read him so wrong? What was going on with him? Maybe it wasn't him. Then it must be her. What was wrong with her? Just when she thought she had matured and was starting to figure out things on her own, this had to happen. Two steps forward and three steps back.

She splashed her face with water once more before leaving the safety of the bathroom stall. A few minutes later, Olive showed up with an extra skip in her step. Great, things were already improving. Not. Can the world just give her ten minutes to herself to breathe?

Olive put an arm around her and whispered into her ear.

"Don't worry, Teal, he's a dud. He probably just wanted to make out with me because Brad told everybody I was easy. Even though we never slept together." Olive tried cheering her up.

She was wasting her time. It wouldn't make a lick of difference. In fact, she only rubbed in the fact that Quinn was interested in Olive and not in her. Nothing would redeem her special night. It was slowly vanishing.

Maybe she was being extra sensitive because of the drinks. Or because it was supposed to have been her one shot with Quinn and it was her birthday. Teal was feeling sorry for herself and this would not help her at all. Once this amazing night was over, she would not be able to take it back. That was the thing about life, you cannot take moments or days back. They disappear forever.

She didn't say anything. She just wanted to be alone, but it didn't seem like that was going to be an option. Even if she could be by herself, she would most likely just go home and veg in front of the TV. No, she couldn't do that because if her mother was home, she would ask questions Teal did not want to answer. So, to avoid that whole scenario, she would have to stay hidden in her bedroom twiddling her thumbs or in a best-case scenario, write in her journal as she collected her tears… until midnight when this would be all be over for good. That might make the night even worse. She couldn't let that happen. Turning sixteen happened only once.

"I know." Olive laughed and grabbed Teal's arm. "Let's go get in line for the Ferris wheel. We'll go on it together! Just you and me. I know you want to. Come on. It will make you feel better."

And they made their way toward the lineup for the ride.

As they waited for their turn, Olive constantly mentioned that Quinn was an idiot. Teal didn't have much of a reply. What could she say? Easy for Olive to say he was an idiot. Quinn liked her. It seemed like guys were always interested in Olive. What was so special about Olive? Teal shook her head again. This was not right. Olive was not being fair. Olive was her best friend. It was not Teal's fault. Besides, she knew what her best friend had that she didn't—the looks. It seemed as though pretty looks were the only thing that mattered those days. Forget that she had good marks, spent time with the elderly (okay, just with Miss Tate but it still counted) and rarely ever gave her parents a hard time. It seemed like that should count for something. She was frustrated to say the least.

"It's our turn!" Olive squealed.

Perhaps Olive had taken too many shots. Teal would try to steer her away from alcohol for the rest of the night.

They hopped onto the seat and were fastened in by a good-looking worker. He was not more than a few years older than Teal and Olive were and smiled at them.

Well, thought Teal, *maybe at us but more in Olive's direction.*

Teal sighed. The night had definitely not turned out the way she'd planned. She had not expected things to be perfect, but this was plain awful. Perhaps "awful" was an understatement?

As the Ferris wheel started moving, Olive rocked the seat back and forth.

"Please, Olive. Don't do that." She liked Ferris wheels but was afraid of heights. She enjoyed the thrill, but saw no reason to tempt fate. Or gravity. Every year she read in the news about a death at some theme park, somewhere, because of a ride of one description or another.

"Oh. You a scaredy-cat? Scaredy-cat!" Olive laughed and laughed at her.

Teal stared back at Olive. Who was this person beside her? Surely it was not her best friend. Olive would never do something like this. She and Olive had been on the Ferris wheel several times before and never had she rocked the seat back and forth. It must have been the booze. It got her. Not a good sign. Not a good feeling at all.

There was not a whole lot Teal could do. She was stuck high in the air and they had just started going around for the second time, so would be stuck together for at least a few more minutes. For sure now, she wanted to go home. And before she started crying in front of Olive. If that happened, it would be a matter of seconds before Olive started calling her a crybaby.

Seriously, this night downright sucked.

Olive stopped rocking the seat, stopped laughing and looked over at Teal, silent for the moment. "I'm sorry. I shouldn't have said that. I don't know what got into me."

Olive grabbed her hand quickly.

With relief, Teal closed her eyes. *This* was Olive. The friend she had known for so many years. On her other hand, Teal secretly crossed her fingers. Maybe a piece of the night could be saved.

Or not! Suddenly she felt something touch her lips and then a tongue was inside her mouth. She opened her eyes quickly.

Olive!

Teal tried to push Olive away. She did not want to embarrass either of them but this was not right. She did not want this. She tried pulling away but the more she tried, the more Olive leaned in, her lips pressed against hers. There was nowhere for her to go.

It seemed like hours, but it was only several seconds that passed. Olive finally let go.

Teal couldn't even look at her. What had just happened? Where was her best friend? Teal looked away, hoping the ride would end sooner than soon.

So much ran through her mind. She had to stay focused. Be on guard. It might be best if she kept her face away from Olive's. Maybe ignore her until the ride was over. Or maybe she had imagined things? She watched the people on the ground. As the ride slowed down, she counted. Five more buckets to go and it would be their turn to get off the ride.

Brad? She glanced down again. Yes, it was Brad. He had been watching the Ferris wheel. Had he seen the kiss? How long had he been watching? As she spotted him for the second time, he darted behind the control booth for his turn on the ride. He seemed to be alone. Maybe he was with his brothers or something. That made sense. A night out with the boys. Except, if it was just that, why had he ducked for cover when she noticed him? The whole thing did not make any sense. Scratch that. The whole *night* had not made any sense.

19

Usually when she entered the apartment, she found Piper in his usual spot on the La-Z-Boy. But tonight, Piper was curled up on her mother's lap, which was unusual. So was the fact that her mother was sitting on the couch and the TV was on and it was way past the 8-p.m. digital and media curfew her mother imposed upon herself every night, including weekends.

"Mom, what's wrong?" Teal dropped the bag and immediately walked to the couch.

Her mother's eyes were watery.

"Accident," her mother sobbed.

"Accident? What accident? Oh my god, is it Dad? Tonya? Toby?"

Her mother shook her head back and forth. Immediately, Teal felt a rush of relief, followed by guilt. Obviously it was not something her mother had read in the newspaper or had seen on the local news. This accident had something to do with someone she knew.

"Sit down, Teal." Her mother patted the cushion beside her.

Teal did not move. She did not need to sit down and talk with her mother. Her mother was behaving strangely. After a moment, though, she felt dizzy and figured it was best to sit, just in case, but as far from her mother as she could. She also wondered if her breath smelled like alcohol. If her mother found out that she had been drinking, things would not get any better from here. In fact, she was sure her mother would never allow her to leave the house again. It was best to listen to her mother when things already seemed off anyway.

"There has been an accident," she explained.

Teal remained silent. This was not news. This she already knew, so she waited.

"Miss Tate was downtown at one of the thrift stores she likes to browse at, probably looking for more frogs to add to her collection. After she left the store, as she crossed the street, a drunk guy from the homeless shelter walked into the middle of traffic. The shelter is only a block away from the thrift store. Cars honked and swerved to avoid hitting him. In all the commotion, a car accidentally hit Miss Tate."

Teal waited for her mother to continue. There was nothing for *her* to say at the moment.

"They rushed her to the hospital right away. But there wasn't anything they could do. She passed away shortly after she got to the hospital. I am so sorry, Teal. She is gone." Her mother started crying all over again.

Teal stared at her. Maybe her mother would stop and

tell her it was only a cruel joke. A couple minutes went by and her mother was still crying.

It was real. Miss Tate was gone. Gone for good.

Teal went to her bedroom where she curled up into a ball on her bed and let the tears flow. At first, she tried to stifle them, then she decided she didn't care who heard her crying. She was in pain. Life would never be the same.

***

Surprisingly, she slept okay. She had expected to be up most of the night, worried and upset about Miss Tate being alone, lying cold somewhere. Of course, Miss Tate was gone and couldn't feel anything, but Teal could imagine.

At the breakfast table, she noticed her mother's eyes were still red. Probably from crying, too. Best not to bring up the subject. Just leave it alone. What was done was done and mentioning it would upset both of them. They would have to figure things out from here on.

"Teal, she had no one. She was all alone."

She didn't have to ask who her mother was talking about. Miss Tate.

"Apparently my contact information was in her wallet in case anything happened to her. She didn't have much family or friends. She has a cousin in Spain, Dottie, who she wrote to regularly, but that was it. She never married. Never had children. That makes it so much worse. She must have been very lonely." Her mother took a sip of tea. "Apparently, I am in charge. I cannot believe I am the executor of her will."

"What? What do you mean? What are you talking about?"

"About six months ago, Miss Tate invited me out to lunch and asked if I could be her executor in case anything happened to her. She was getting older and wanted to make sure everything was in place." Her mother shook her head in awe. "But I never thought she would really leave us."

"Okay." Teal wasn't sure what to say. She was surprised her mother had never mentioned the lunch and the executor of the will thing before this. The loss of Miss Tate would be felt for a long time. As for her mother being the executor of the will, it wouldn't really have an effect on Teal.

"I am going over to her apartment to open the will and start making a list of things that need to be done. Do you want to do come with me? It will be creepy being in her apartment without her. This is only my third time visiting her place."

Teal didn't have to think about it. It would feel too weird being in Miss Tate's apartment without her there. Like invading her privacy. It would just be wrong.

"I can't." She got up from the table and went to her room.

"That's where I'll be if you need me. Or if you change your mind."

Teal waited for the apartment door to close, meaning her mother had left for Miss Tate's, but it was at least half an hour or longer before it finally did. She felt bad. Her mother probably thought she would change her mind.

***

After sitting on the bed for quite some time, Teal decided to write a sympathy letter to Miss Tate's cousin, Dottie. She wanted to let her know how special Miss Tate was and how much her friendship had meant. She was missing Miss Tate already.

She had only meant to write a few lines. After writing the condolences though, she had felt the need to keep writing and so she did. She shared some of her memories. The letter even included how and when she and Miss Tate had become friends. She even admitted, that at first, she thought of Miss Tate as the grumpy lady next door. Maybe Dottie would write back. Maybe not. The important thing was for Dottie to know how special Miss Tate had been to Teal. That Miss Tate had not been completely alone. There was no way of knowing, of course, if Dottie would write back, or if she would even care. Teal had done her part.

20

With Piper in hand and the letter to Dottie to mail, Teal trailed slowly along the sidewalk. Piper seemed to sense the mood and was quieter than usual. Teal had hoped, by walking and walking, she could somehow feel better. It was hard to believe that just a few days ago, life had seemed decent. She had been getting ready to celebrate her birthday, her father had announced he was getting married and adopting Toby. Now this. It was too much.

It seemed as though each time she got a grip on something, her life took a turn and convinced her otherwise. Would it always be like this? When she was an actual adult, would things be different? Maybe it was best not to think about it.

The previous evening, Olive had sent three text messages begging for a reply. Teal had read them, of course, but wasn't interested in responding at the moment. Although a big part of that was because she didn't know what to say. They had known each other for a long time. Teal was still in disbelief. Olive could wait. Teal was in no rush to talk about what had taken place on the Ferris wheel.

"Hey. If you looked up you'd see where you're going."

Teal had nearly bumped into him.

"And now that you have looked up, I can see your pretty eyes." Jackson smiled.

"Sorry about that. I have a lot on my mind. I thought going for a walk might help." She kept walking toward the park near the courthouse. It was one of her favorite places. There was lots of grass, benches and a water fountain. The perfect place to be alone or with your dog. Piper loved coming here. As soon as Piper realized they were close to the park, he tugged on his leash as if to let her know she was walking too slowly for his liking.

Jackson kept up the pace. For several moments, they walked in silence. Fine by her. She was not really in a talking mood but somehow felt comforted with Jackson by her side.

At the park, she went to her favorite bench and sat. Piper lay down beside her on the grass. He seemed content enough, he stayed still but his eyes watched everything going on around him.

Jackson sat beside her.

She looked at him with no idea of what to say, but it was nice he was there with her. She did not feel like being alone.

Jackson remained silent.

Eventually, she decided to start some sort of conversation before things became awkward between them. In addition, she hoped he would not mention the party. The last thing she needed right now was to find out she was the laughing stock of the school.

Before she could start a conversation, Jackson did.

"I am really sorry about Miss Tate, Teal." Was Jackson waiting for a reaction?

"How did you find out?" It was not as though she had told anyone. Not even her best friend, Olive.

"My mom told me about what happened. I know you spent time with Miss Tate. When you could. Like going over to her place for tea and what not. That was sweet of you. Most girls wouldn't do something like that." He smiled.

"I'm not sure I know what you mean." *What was he talking about?*

"Most girls are usually on social media, out with friends and stuff. Not usually volunteering their time with an elderly woman and sipping tea." He laughed.

Was he making fun of her? Better to tread softly. But she liked his laugh. She wanted to hear it again. Maybe she would get to.

She smiled back. For the first time since she'd heard the news of Miss Tate, her heart had not felt like an elephant was sitting on it. This was definitely a good sign.

***

After she returned home from the walk with Piper, she did, in fact, feel better. She was not ready to attempt cartwheels just yet but still… it was progress. She had enjoyed spending time with Jackson. She didn't know him all that well, but he seemed nice. He had given her space and had made small talk, both of which she had needed. Sitting around her room had not helped at all. She didn't want to hang out in the living room either because she was afraid her mother would worry about her, or bother her with questions. Teal was not in the mood to deal with anything of the kind just yet.

Normally, Teal would have gone over to Olive's to talk with her, but she didn't want to. Olive would try to pull every detail out of her regarding the accident. That was fine for funny situations—or embarrassing ones—but not for something like this. Not when her heart ached. She would also love to tell her about Jackson. How they had spent some time together and how he had even asked for her phone number. That they were supposed to make plans to meet up again soon. How she was looking forward to it. That maybe this would go somewhere. But she did not want to tell Olive in case Olive wrecked things. It sounded mean, but she didn't trust Olive when it came to people, not that she personally had a lot of experience herself. There was a chance Olive would also mention the kiss and that would make things really awkward. Olive was aware of the friend code, but did not always stick with it. That was a huge difference for sure!

But now, she actually felt good enough to reply to Olive's messages. And she'd better do it right now before the mood passed and things lingered on. It would not get any easier. In fact, things would only get more complicated the longer she waited it out.

> Why did you do that?-T
>
> Do what?-O
>
> Isn't that what you are saying sorry about?-T
>
> I am not sure what you are talking about.-O

It was just like Olive to start playing games when things really counted. It was so frustrating being friends with her at times. No way she would let it go so easily.

> The Ferris wheel. What happened when we were on the Ferris wheel?-T
>
> I had fun. Didn't you?-O
>
> Um, no. I don't know why you would do such a thing.-T
>
> I didn't do anything. I am not sure what you're talking about.-O
>
> So what are you sorry for?-T
>
> Miss Tate. I called and your mom told me about what happened.-O

All right, the conversation made a little more sense now but not by a lot.

It looked like Olive was going to skip over the incident.

Fine, Olive could have this one.

Teal tried one last time and then left it alone. She did not have the energy to argue with Olive. They had been friends for a long time so maybe the incident would disappear into thin air, never to be spoken of again. She hoped so. She did not want to give Olive the wrong impression.

> Why did you try and kiss me on the Ferris wheel?-T

> I didn't try to kiss you. WE kissed.-O

What was Olive doing? Was she trying to blame Teal? Or imply that it was a joint idea for the kiss? That was definitely not what had happened. She remembered Olive as she had leaned in, kissed her and trying to get her to stop. Which Olive first refused to do.

> Olive. I like you as a friend.-T

No response. Five minutes later she tried again.

> This is silly. We are best friends. Please don't be mad.-T

Even after texting about what had happened, things were still as clear as mud. Teal pretended she wasn't watching her phone as she waited for Olive to message back, but that wasn't working.

After half an hour, she gave up and tried to keep herself busy to take her mind off the situation. It took a lot of effort.

The next morning, Teal checked the phone. Olive had not replied. This was not a good sign for sure. Not much could be done about it, though. She had meant what she said and she had plenty of other things to deal with. Like Miss Tate. She crossed her fingers that down the road things would work themselves out. That Olive would come around. She just had to.

21

TEAL SQUEALED.

It had arrived! The envelope was magnificent. She traced her right index finger along the gold filigree writing with her name on it. She opened the envelope slowly and slid the invitation out. It was actually going to happen. Her father was getting married to Tonya. Best of all was the fact that she was okay with it. It had taken her a while to realize that her parents were not getting back together. She would also be the first to admit that she and Tonya had not exactly got off on the right foot. But slowly, over time, they had given each other a chance. Her father was happy, and Teal was happy, and involved. This was all she had wanted in the first place. No one ever wanted to feel left out or replaced.

The moment she entered the living room, her mother rose to block the computer's screen.

"I'm not sure what you're up to, Mom, but you can

relax. It's not like I can ground you or anything."

She waved the wedding invitation around. She wasn't paying attention to what her mother was doing. Right now, it was all about the wedding.

"Oh. The invitation came. That's great. I'll bet you're excited." Her mother took a step back which covered the computer's screen even more. "It's nothing really."

"You would win the bet. Dad is getting married and I get to be part of the wedding party!"

Teal continued waving the invite to be sure her mother saw how amazing it looked.

Then she stopped. How could she be so insensitive? Here was her father moving on with his life. He had pretty much a stepson and was getting married to someone he loved. And as far as she knew, her mother had not even been out on a date since the breakup. Then again, that wasn't saying much, because she doubted her mother would even mention something like that to her. If her mother ended up seeing someone regularly, she might. But not in the beginning.

"When I said 'it's nothing really,' I wasn't talking about the wedding. I've been somewhat bored lately so I thought I'd take an online course. Just for something to do. Not even sure why I'm bringing it up."

"That's okay. But now you *are* acting kind of strange. Name one person who takes an online course just for something to do. I guess that's what happens when you get older. What course are you taking?"

She slid the card back inside the pretty envelope, planning to paste it inside her journal as a souvenir. Teal felt awesome about the wedding invitation so wasn't really interested in hearing about the course her mother was taking; but thought she should at least ask about it.

"Well, I don't want to jinx it or anything, so no worries." Her mother closed the computer. Just like that. Her mother's actions looked even more suspicious now. A red flag for sure.

Teal waited to see if her mother was going to say anything else. When she didn't, Teal went to her room. Maybe if she wrote a few pages in her journal it would make her feel better about Olive. And maybe Jackson would be in touch. She smiled. Maybe things would improve in the next while. First, though, she had to get through the funeral arrangements for Miss Tate. She had never been to a funeral before. This was a first so she wondered what it would be like. Would anyone besides her and her mother attend? It would be sad if it was just the two of them. Surely Miss Tate had touched at least a few other people in her life.

Tears slipped down over Teal's cheeks and onto the page of her journal. She wiped them away. It was hard to believe Miss Tate was gone. It would be weird not to visit her anymore. They had become close over the last few months. Teal wouldn't have anyone to confide in anymore. There was Olive, but it wasn't the same. Especially since sometimes, it was Olive she needed to talk about.

22

As she entered the apartment, Teal called out to see if her mother was home.

No one replied.

In her room, she placed her cell phone on the charger and quickly checked each room in the apartment. She was alone. Good that her mother was out doing something. But since Teal didn't know where she was, that meant she didn't have any idea what time her mother would be home, so how much time she had to do what she wanted to do. Now was the time though. She had to be quick.

She sat down at the computer and turned it on. Her mother's password to log on was T-E-A-L. She knew that. In less than thirty seconds, she was in. If her mother suddenly arrived home and asked what she was doing, she would simply say that her laptop had acted up. She immediately put the cursor on the browsing history. All the sites listed had to do with checking on people, like spying on them.

She clicked on a few more of the sites and came up with the same information. This had nothing to do with online dating or anything of that sort. The entire browsing history had to do with private investigating. This couldn't be the kind of course her mother had talked about.

What was her mother up to? Her father? That had to be it. Her mother investigating her father and Tonya. It had to be something like that. Unless her mother had someone spying on her! What for though? This wasn't making any sense at all. Her mother was the one who had filed for divorce and had seemed okay with everything, including when her father had started dating Tonya. Had Teal been wrong? Was her mother secretly seething about her father finding someone to share his life with and moving on without her? That didn't sound like her mother but then again, she doubted that her mother would have said anything to her in the first place. No wonder her mother hadn't been excited about the wedding invite. It was all starting to make sense now.

Teal turned off the computer and went back to her room to write in her journal. All right, so now she knew what her mother had been doing. Mystery solved. Unfortunately, now there were a couple more mysteries. Who had her mother hired to spy for her? Why were they spying? Probably on her father. If so, did her father not have a right to know? But after she received the wedding invitation and everything, she wasn't sure this would be the time to tell him. On the other hand, he should know if her mother was trying to sabotage the wedding—if that was in fact the case. Damn it. She needed to give it some more thought before she made a decision. If it wasn't one thing, it was another.

23

Teal prepared herself for the funeral. She had gone shopping with her mother to find a plain black dress to wear for the last goodbye to Miss Tate. Strange how she would attend her first funeral and first wedding within the same year. It didn't seem right. It did not seem appropriate. No. Maybe that wasn't the word she was looking for. Nevertheless, something was off. She had even Googled what to expect with regards to funerals but there had been an excessive amount of variations depending on a person's wishes, family preferences, cost, and culture, among other things.

Teal's mother had picked out a mint-green coffin because of Miss Tate's fondness for frogs. There would be a viewing that afternoon and the following evening, then Miss Tate would be buried the day after that. Teal didn't want to think of Miss Tate being alone so planned to be there for each step of this unfamiliar process.

Another reason she wanted to be there was to support her mother. She'd been unable to help out with the funeral arrangements because of school. Today was different. She wouldn't be going to school.

When she entered the funeral home, Teal was surprised to see that everything looked like a fancy living room with comfortable chairs along the walls and carpeting on the floor. On the chair nearest the coffin sat an elderly woman.

This woman looked younger than Miss Tate and they shared the same big nose. Her gray hair had been swept up into an old-fashioned bun just as Miss Tate had always worn her hair. This woman had to be Dottie, Miss Tate's cousin. Teal was sure of it. She didn't know everyone in the neighborhood on a first name basis, most only by sight, but for sure, this woman was not one of them.

When Teal hugged her mother, she asked about the woman. Her mother confirmed that the lady was, in fact, Dottie.

Teal approached her.

Dottie stood up and smiled. "Thanks for your letter. It was sweet and thoughtful of you."

Teal blinked. *Really?* "I didn't think you'd get it that fast." She'd paid extra to make sure it wouldn't take weeks to arrive, yes, but this was quicker than she'd expected. She'd included a condolence card as well as the letter. Cards, she'd learned from her online research, should be received *after* a family member has passed away. This was embarrassing.

Dottie sat back down. "I hope you don't mind if I sit,

dear. It was quite the trip getting here and my legs aren't as young as they used to be."

Teal chose the chair to the right of Dottie, glad it wasn't the one right beside the coffin as Dottie's was. "No worries. I bet the plane ride was long. I've never been on a plane." This, she offered by way of conversation because she couldn't think of anything else to say but felt as though she owed it to Miss Tate to make an effort. She'd be here for at least two more hours so had to start somewhere.

"You're young. Still lots of time for a plane ride."

"I haven't even really been out of Ottawa yet. I hope that someday I can travel outside Canada. That would be fun." Funny, she had never thought of traveling outside of the province before. Now suddenly, here she was, talking about taking an airplane to another country. Interesting how things could change so quickly at special times.

As they continued to chat, Teal kept an eye out for other guests who seemed familiar. When she would see someone she knew, she would approach them and chat for a minute or two before returning to Dottie's side to pick up the conversation where they'd left off.

Half an hour into the viewing, Olive showed up with her mother. Teal wasn't quite sure how she was going to handle this. She and Olive had not spoken to each other, or texted, since Teal had sent that final message stating she liked Olive only as a friend. It still bothered her a lot that Olive had not taken the time to respond, but had just let things go at that. They'd been together as friends for such a long time. Teal had no idea what was going on with Olive, but she didn't like it one bit. There was always something or other going on in Teal's life, but she'd had Olive as her one constant. Things had not always run smoothly but she couldn't ever remember things being this strained. Although the time she had told Olive that Brad was cheating on her was definitely comparable. Maybe their friendship was being tested? More importantly, if that was the case, could their friendship survive?

As Teal rose to make her way over to Olive, Olive started in her direction. Teal decided to stand still. Best to let Olive come to her. Maybe if she stayed near Dottie there would no way Olive would make a scene. Not that she thought her friend would do such a thing. Or would she? Maybe she wouldn't have in the past, but things were different now. Teal was confused. She didn't know where the two of them stood.

Teal introduced them. "This is Dottie, Miss Tate's cousin."

"My condolences, Dottie. I met Miss Tate a couple of times. A nice lady." Olive gave Dottie one of her award-winning smiles.

Olive probably had not wanted to attend the wake, even though it was just for a few minutes out of respect for Teal and Teal's mother. That was the thing with Olive sometimes, if she wasn't personally involved, she wouldn't make an effort. Teal wondered if it had always been like this.

It might be best just to give Olive permission to leave. She could do that much. She enjoyed Dottie's company and every so often, she saw her mother look over in her direction to make sure she was okay.

Teal reached over and gave Olive a big hug.

"Thanks for coming, Olive, it means a lot." She smiled. She'd made the effort.

Olive leaned forward to whisper in Teal's left ear.

"You liked it." Then she quickly pulled away. "I'll message you later, Teal. Take care of yourself now." Olive winked and walked away.

Teal stood there too dumbfounded to move. How could Olive say such a thing? Not to mention that Olive reeked of alcohol. Had her own mother not noticed? It was a weekday afternoon. Teal shook her head. Olive was not her problem now. Best to stay in the present and continue with Dottie. She was worried though. This was not a good sign for Olive, or for Teal. It would be only a matter of time before Teal would be dragged into Olive's mess of a life.

24

DOTTIE CONTINUED TALKING.

"I appreciate the card and even more so, your letter. It was from the heart. It was genuine. You don't see enough of that these days. Especially from the younger generation. I don't mean anything bad by that. I am just stating an observation, an opinion. Today, people want to send messages over a phone or talk for thirty seconds. No one takes the time to visit or write letters or be honest with each other. No one wants to hurt anyone's feelings. People are even suing each other over silly matters. It does not make a lick of sense to me. That's fine and dandy for some folks but that's not the real world. Children need to be allowed to be children, to play outside, learn to ride a bicycle at the age of three instead of playing on those pad things. At the mall the other day, I even saw a woman pushing a double stroller. In the stroller was a baby, no more than a couple of months old,

I'd say, and a toddler young enough to be in diapers. The baby was asleep, but the toddler was trying to get the woman's attention. But no. The woman was too busy on her phone. There she was, pushing the stroller with one hand and tapping rapidly with her thumb on the other hand. I don't know. What do you call it? Texting? Or, maybe even playing a game. Either way, she was in her own little world. And there was her child, essentially alone." Dottie shook her head. "I don't think things will get better with time. Sad. But this is the real world of today and this is where I live right now. Right here inside the real world. Right here." She pointed her right index finger toward the floor to indicate the exact spot where her feet were.

Teal stifled a small laugh but failed miserably. Even if she'd had some preconceived notion of what Dottie's character would be, this hadn't been it. She was even more feisty than Miss Tate had been! What a hoot. She couldn't imagine how things might have gone if she'd had the opportunity to have tea with both Dottie and Miss Tate.

"Good. I made you laugh," said Dottie, smiling up at her. "That's another thing. There's not enough laughter in the world. It's the best medicine, you know. And it's still free. Imagine that. Strange how some folks don't want any of it."

***

Throughout the rest of the wake, Teal checked in with other people who came to pay their respects to Miss Tate but her mother was doing well with that part so Teal let her deal with it. Instead, she found herself sipping tea (and this time it almost tasted like Miss Tate's tea) and digestive cookies as she continued to chat with Dottie. They talked about Miss Tate's newfound obsession with frogs; Miss Tate's tasty tea; and a prank the girls had once pulled on one of their male cousins at a Sunday picnic after church.

As everyone began trickling out, Dottie rummaged around in her purse to retrieve a small frog, maybe an inch in size. Her eyes meet with Teal's. She winked.

"I know she started collecting frogs recently. I wanted to make sure she had one to take with her to keep her company." Dottie glanced around to make sure no one was looking their way, then dropped the frog into the coffin beside Miss Tate.

Teal couldn't believe what she had just seen. She should mention the frog to her mother just in case any questions were asked. Tell her that nothing fishy was going on, just a little frog to keep Miss Tate company on her journey. In some of the articles she'd read on the Internet, she learned that family members often put a variety of things inside their loved ones' coffins before it was sealed shut. People placed wedding rings, a necklace, a watch, teddy bears, pictures, with their loved ones, just to name a few things.

Dottie hugged her.

Their eyes locked again. "Promise me something?"

Teal had just met the woman. She couldn't think of one possible thing she could offer this elderly woman. Not to mention they lived in separate countries. An ocean separated them. What could she say? She owed it to Miss Tate to hear Dottie out.

"Okay. Uh."

Dottie smiled. "Take that worried look off your face."

Teal tried to relax, but she still wasn't sure what Dottie wanted from her.

"Keep in touch is all I'm asking of you. Please keep in contact by letter. When I received that letter you sent, it made my heart melt. It felt good. I liked the feeling and I want to feel it again and again, if possible. I do not get much mail anymore, except for flyers. It's not like my younger days when I would rush out to the mail to get colorful catalogs, letters from friends, news from the rest of the world and other items. Everything is online now. It's fast and fun for window shopping but I do miss my mail, especially letters from my family. And now I don't have anyone left. My cousin was the last one." Dottie's eyes welled up with tears.

Of course, of course she would do this one thing for Dottie. "I will try my best to write a letter to you at least once a month."

"Thanks. My cousin really cared about you and looked forward to your visits. It meant a lot that a teenage girl, in this day and age, would spend time with her. And you're not even family." She pointed to the entrance way where a man stood. "Oh. There's my taxi. Take care of yourself, Teal." Dottie made her way out the door.

Teal made it through the funeral and it looked like she had a new pen pal. She hoped Dottie would write back. Getting mail from another country would be cool. Of course, she was still upset that Miss Tate was gone, but Dottie was an unexpected gift and she would take it. Dottie could never replace Miss Tate but perhaps another adventure was just around the corner. It seemed strange at first but by the end, she had felt comfort from Dottie's company. It felt good to laugh and have someone else to talk with. She did not have many people around her now, especially since Miss Tate was gone and she and Olive weren't on the best of terms.

25

Jackson was two years older than she was. He didn't have milk-chocolate eyes but his were a deep sea green that went perfectly with his dark blonde hair. He was exactly six feet tall and that worked out well because Teal preferred taller guys.

They had kept in touch.

She didn't want to get her hopes up, but she was starting to fall for him, finding herself checking her cell phone more than usual in case he'd sent a message and she hadn't heard the notification. And here they were together. Jackson and Teal were sitting under a big oak tree with a light-yellow blanket spread out before them. They had decided to have a make-shift picnic, but instead of making sandwiches, they had stopped at a Subway on their way to grab a sub combo each. Jackson had chosen the turkey club and she'd picked the Italian BMT combo. He chose regular chips and she chose macadamia cookies. Turned out he liked Coke and she liked Sprite.

"Is this okay?" Jackson asked.

"Perfect. It's nice out and there won't be a mess to clean up after we're done eating either." She smiled.

"I can't remember if it's my turn or yours to ask a question." Jackson looked at Teal.

"It's mine and I have thought about it. My question is, I would like to know if you have any piercings or tattoos that I can't see." She had noticed his ears were not pierced. She couldn't see any tattoos either but then again, he was fully clothed. Lots of body canvas was still covered. That was how Teal liked to think of the human body.

"No piercings. I thought about it a few times but then the thought would somehow just go away so I don't think it's something I really want at this point. No rush. It may never happen. As for tattoos, I do have one. Got it before my eighteenth birthday." Jackson raised his eyebrows and smiled.

"Are you serious? I don't believe you. You have to show me." She accidentally let out a small squeal.

Jackson took a bite of sandwich and stared at her, waiting.

Teal waited, too. She wouldn't ask again.

Jackson took the last bite of his sub, used a napkin to wipe his mouth and hands. Smiling, he bent down, unlaced his left shoe and took it off. Next came his sock. She watched, wondering what was next. He was probably tricking her or something. Why else would he be taking off his socks and shoes? She couldn't think of anything. Maybe he really liked the way grass felt on his bare feet and he was going to walk around or something. Strange… but she could deal with it.

After he removed the sock, Jackson turned his foot toward her so she could see the other side of it. He had a tattoo there. A small black one. It was some sort of oriental style writing located just above his toes. She couldn't believe it. It was cool. Jackson was neat. She had never thought he would have tattoos.

"Pretty neat but what does the writing mean?"

"It means love in Japanese. When my dad was really sick, before he passed away of lung cancer, I spent a lot of time with him and my mom. After he was gone, it was just Mom and me. As strange as it sounds, I wanted something to remember him and our family as it had been. Mom and I don't agree on a lot of things, but we respect each other, and we make the effort to spend time doing things together. I got along with both my parents before my dad started getting sick. But after he died… Well… That changed everything." Jackson looked down at his foot.

She had known Jackson's father was not around but not why. It was something you just didn't ask about. It was assumed that if someone's father wasn't in the picture, it was because he had taken off, or the parents were divorced so the person didn't have contact with their father. It was very rare that it might be because the parent had passed away. It was sad. Until today, she had figured his father had run off and left his mother for someone else or he had not wanted to be a father. In her experience, that was why a parent wasn't in the picture, they simply did not want to be a parent.

"How long has it been?" Teal asked. When no reply came, she continued, "If you don't want to talk about it or anything that's fine."

"Dad had only been gone for about a month when I decided I really wanted to get it done. I kept bugging Mom all day and night, day after day. Finally, after several months she relented, just as long as I promised to shut up afterward." Jackson laughed. "She told me I was going to give her white hair." He put his sock back on. "It hasn't been quite a year. Mom had to come with me and sign a consent form because I wasn't eighteen yet. She was pretty cool about the whole thing." He put on his shoe. "Even after she said yes, she made me think about it for six months to make sure I really wanted to have it done. I was not too happy about waiting all that time but now I can kind of see her point. It's not like these things have an expiry date or are done with a Sharpie." His tattoo was again no longer visible.

"I wouldn't mind getting a tattoo. Maybe later down the road. I'm not really sure what I would get done yet." She giggled. Where had that come from? She had never even thought about getting a tattoo before now. Look at how the nose-piercing had turned out. It hadn't. She'd thought about it and thought about it but in the end, could not go through with it. A nose-piercing was nowhere nearly as permanent as a tattoo.

Strange, but when she was with Jackson, she felt better about herself. More mature, confident, and full of ideas that seemed out character for her. Like thinking about getting a tattoo.

Teal's phone buzzed.

> Brad wants to get back together.-O
>
> Okay.-T
>
> Should I meet up with him to talk?-O
>
> Are you going to go back with him?-T
>
> Um, I'm not sure.-O
>
> It's up to you.-T

Why did Olive even bother to message her? Whatever Olive wanted to do, she did. Most of the time, whatever mess Olive was currently standing in, it was her own doing and yet she expected other people to bail her out.

Of course she did not believe Olive would go back to Brad. Olive had to know that Brad was crazy. He had cheated on Olive with Trina. He had even tried to get Teal to convince Olive to take him back, and to tell Olive it had all been a misunderstanding. The guy had issues. Olive had enough trouble of her own. Adding him to the mix spelled D-I-S-A-S-T-E-R. If they did get back together, it would be just a matter of time before everything boiled over again.

Teal could do nothing but wait.

Teal couldn't believe it. Olive had messaged her. Olive was thinking about getting back together with Brad. It was not a good idea and Olive should know that, too. Well, it was Olive's decision, wasn't it? Maybe she would get back with Brad or maybe she wouldn't.

Right now, Teal needed to push her friend out of her

mind and stay focused on the present. Currently the present included Jackson, not Olive.

Strange though, Olive had not really been in touch with her since the little incident at the funeral for Miss Tate. Maybe Olive was too embarrassed? Maybe Olive didn't want to acknowledge what she had done? Was that partly Teal's own fault because she never confronted Olive when things like this happened? Because she always let Olive get away with things? Then there was the incident at the funeral. Teal didn't know what to think. Either Olive would deny what she'd said or would act like Teal was okay with what happened. Olive never dwelled on the past. Was that a good or a bad thing?

Sometimes Teal wished she could be more like that. She was the one who usually got upset. Not Olive. But right now, it wasn't worth it. She should just let it go. If Olive didn't want to bring it up and talk about it, then neither would she. Maybe in some bizarre way, Olive was purposely trying to upset her or something.

"Sorry about that. A friend wanted my opinion on something." She smiled and took in a deep breath. Time to focus on the present and the good things.

"That's cool." Jackson's eyes met hers.

"Not really, she's going to do the exact opposite of what I said." Teal started cleaning up the empty wrappers and used serviettes from the subs. At least Jackson hadn't been annoyed while she replied to Olive's text. Not that she was always on her phone or anything, but she knew some guys who would get annoyed when girls sent someone a text while they were together. It was like they thought they were the only person in the world.

Jackson laughed. "That's usually how it goes with friendships or relationships with parents."

Teal just might be onto something. Jackson was wise and sure did pack a punch. She was starting to like him more and more.

26

Teal finished writing in her journal for the night and was getting ready for bed when she received a message from Olive.

> I didn't respond to Brad's message.
>
> I just ignored it.
>
> But he just sent me another message saying he cannot and will not be ignored like this.
>
> I am not going to respond.-O

She was impressed that Olive hadn't met up with Brad nor taken him back. Maybe Olive was learning to at least think things through more. A good sign. Perhaps she was starting to mature.

Teal responded quickly.

> Awesome. I am proud of you! Hopefully he will take the hint now!-T

Brad's strategy didn't seem too brilliant, saying he wouldn't be ignored then expecting Olive to meet up with him. Hopefully Brad would leave things alone now. Leave both of them alone. For good.

27

Tonya handed Teal another wedding catalog. Several pages were marked.

"I thought maybe you could help decide what colors we would use in the wedding. What do you think?" Tonya asked with a smile.

Teal had to stay focused. She would worry about her mother's hiring a spy later when back at home. There wasn't any point in ruining her weekend stressing over it. Besides, looking at wedding stuff with Tonya was kind of fun. Another first. Being included felt good. "I would love to have something in a shade of purple, whatever you think might match. If that's okay with you."

"I'm sure we can find something we both like, and Toby's suit will be the same color, to match. I was wondering if it would be okay if he could walk down the aisle with you. You two would be holding hands. If you're not comfortable with that, no worries. He can walk down the aisle with me or with your dad. I don't want you to feel any pressure about anything."

Just then Teal's phone buzzed. It was a message from Olive. She ignored it. She would read and respond to it later.

"Honestly? I would love to have Toby walk down the aisle with me. It would be so cute." She meant it. It would be neat being the center of attention for once and she knew Toby would melt everyone's heart. They wouldn't be able to help it.

Just then, Toby entered the living room. As soon as he saw Teal, he made a beeline in her direction.

"Tee!" Toby squealed as he hopped onto the couch beside her.

She smiled. He was not only cute but he was well-behaved. Especially now that he was toilet trained. Not that she had to change his diapers all that often. Her father and Tonya had been pretty good about that. They had never asked her to change diapers except for when she was paid to babysit the odd time and that was fine with her.

Her cell phone went off again. Yet another message from Olive. She didn't read it. She was busy. Olive could wait. Olive needed to learn that Teal wasn't always going to be around to jump when she said jump.

"Take a look at the pages I marked. See if any ideas jump out at you. No pressure," Tonya smiled at her. "But it would be easier if we could tag team your dad together."

Teal liked the idea of tag-teaming her father. There

was no way her father could say no to both of them if they wanted the same thing. It would be undemocratic and mean, wouldn't it?

"Good idea," she said.

28

Toby had just flipped to the last page of the book she was reading to him, a Little Golden Book titled *The Poky Little Puppy*, when her cell went off for a third time. This time, Olive hadn't sent a message, she was calling. Teal quickly finished reading the book. Toby took off to his room running to put the book away and no doubt find another one to be read.

Teal answered the phone.

"Help!" Olive screamed.

"What? What's going on? Are you hurt?" Teal got up off the couch.

"It's Brad. He's trying to get inside the house. I'm home alone!"

"What? He's trying to break into your house? Are all the doors locked?" While talking, she threw things into a bag. She had to get to Olive.

She could feel Tonya watching her every move.

"The doors are locked but I think he's trying to break the glass door." Teal could hear Olive sobbing with fear.

Teal heard a commotion in the background.

"I'm on my way. I'll call the police. Just stay where you are."

Teal hung up the phone.

"Do you want me to drive you over?" Tonya asked.

"Thanks but it would be quicker if I just ran over. But could you call the police for me?" She scribbled Olive's address on one of the catalogs on the coffee table.

"I will. Be safe." Tonya hugged Teal quickly before she left.

***

By the time Teal arrived at Olive's front door, she was out of breath. She pounded furiously on Olive's front door. She tried to go in, but it was locked. Of course it was. She had told Olive to do so. What if Brad was already in the house with Olive? Her heart raced. She should have let Tonya come with her but what would Tonya have done with Toby? She'd been silly to think she could handle something like this on her own. Thoughtless.

She pounded on the door again. "It's me, Olive. It's me. Teal. Open the door."

No answer. Olive had known she was on her way.

"Olive! The police are on their way. I called them. Can you hear me?"

This wasn't happening. She continued to pound on the door.

Suddenly, Olive opened the door so fast, she nearly

did a face plant into the carpet.

"Quick! Come in."

"Lock it. Lock it now!" Teal yelled.

"Olive, I want answers. And I want them now." Brad hollered from somewhere.

Teal was shocked when she heard Brad. Things started to become more real.

Staring at each other, they stood motionless by the front door, too paralyzed to move.

Teal concentrated for a few seconds but as much as she tried, she couldn't hear any police sirens. What was taking them so long?

It felt like it had been hours since she'd left her father's house.

Glass shattered.

"I just want to know why!" Brad yelled.

"Don't answer him, Olive. No matter what you say, it won't be the answer he wants to hear." Teal warned.

"I'm sorry!" Olive yelled back.

Teal shook her head. Olive was making things worse. Teal clenched her fist. All she wanted to do was slap Olive or shake some sense into her. Olive would never learn.

They heard more glass break, and pounding at the back door.

A commotion at the front door made them whirl around.

"Police! Open up. Police. Open up now!"

Teal's hands trembled as she fiddled with the doorknob. She tried to speak but words would not come out. Instead, she pointed toward the back of the house. By then, the police officers, two six-foot-tall, well-built men, didn't need directions. They followed the sound of glass shattering and Brad himself.

Olive clung to her. They stood, didn't move or speak. A couple of minutes later two female police officers arrived.

"Are you okay?" The taller one asked.

Olive and Teal nodded their heads yes.

The other police officer guided Olive over to sit on the couch.

"Take your time. Stay here for a minute to catch your breath. When you're ready, you can explain what happened. Every detail you can think of. After you tell me what happened, I'll go over everything one more time but with me asking questions. That way, you might end up giving me more information. You might remember something else. Let's start with the man at the door. Apparently, you know who he is?"

Just as Olive was about to speak, there was another commotion at the back of the house.

The two male police officers were with Brad back in the kitchen. Olive's eyes widened when she saw the handcuffs on Brad.

Teal reached for Olive's hand, trying to distract her.

As Olive watched Brad moving through the house in handcuffs, this seemed to upset her even more. This was the last thing everyone needed. Olive had to focus on telling the police officer what had happened so they could deal with the situation.

Olive managed to get out two full sentences before Brad yelled again

"It's your fault. How could you sleep with him? I love you!"

Brad was talking about Tank, of course. The last guy Olive had been with after Brad. Tank and Olive had been together for nearly five months. They broke up because Tank got a job at a gas station and started seeing less and less of Olive.

The police led Brad out the door.

29

For the past two days, Jackson had asked the same question again and again. "Are you sure you want to do this?"

And Teal had given him the same answer again and again. Yes. She was sure.

She had decided to get a small tattoo in memory of Miss Tate. Just a small one. She would make sure it was covered so her mother or father wouldn't see it. She knew she wouldn't be able to hide the tattoo forever. But if she could at least keep it hidden until she became the legal age to get one done without her parents' permission, then perhaps her parents would go easier on her. Maybe she would live to tell the tale.

The age to get a tattoo without having one of your parents or a legal guardian sign for you was eighteen. She was sixteen, so that meant it was possible for her to get a tattoo if someone else signed for her. After making the decision to get one, the next step was figuring out how to get around the signature part.

Teal made sure to do research about getting a tattoo and knew enough not to let some drunk guy in a basement, with the nickname Tiny do it. The tattoo she had picked out was super cute. It was about the size of a quarter and she planned to have it done on her left foot.

To get a tattoo session arranged, Jackson had approached a friend of his, Tran, the tattoo artist who had done Jackson's tattoo, to see what options he could suggest, if any.

Tran said he didn't want me going to anyone in a dark basement either. And, at first Tran had resisted. In fact, he had flat out said no. He said there was no way he would do it without one of Teal's parents present and watching them sign the release form.

Eventually, though, Jackson had broken him down. Jackson paid twice the amount the tattoo would normally have cost and promised not to let anyone know Tran was breaking the rules. In return, Tran would do the tattoo himself and look the other way.

All Teal had to do, Tran insisted, was bring proper ID so he could make a copy as was his usual practice.

Jackson would have to bring his as well, and on the parent or guardian section, Jackson would sign.

Even though it had been planned out for a while and she had known what to expect, as they walked into the tattoo place her heart beat faster.

Tran had arranged to have her and Jackson come an hour after the shop had closed for the night. That way, there wouldn't be any witnesses. That was the actual word Tran had used. It seemed to make him feel better.

This didn't work so well for her viewpoint, though. There would be no one to witness if anything went wrong. The night before her appointment, she actually had a nightmare in which, after getting the tattoo done, she removed the bandage and instead of the tattoo she wanted, the word *Loser* had been permanently tattooed on her foot. It wasn't enough to scare her away or change her mind, though. She would go through with it for Miss Tate.

When they arrived at the shop, Jackson pulled on the door. It was locked, as expected. Jackson quickly dialed Tran's number.

A few seconds later Tran was at the door, all smiles.

"Almost show time." He grinned.

Tran handed the sheet for consent over and took both hers and Jackson's ID to make photocopies of them.

"I am going to ask this one last time. Are you sure?" Jackson asked, touching her right shoulder.

"Yes, I am sure and no I won't blame you if I have any regrets. Don't worry. I'm making this decision on my own. I'm my own person." Teal touched his hand.

Jackson was wonderful. She honestly didn't feel any pressure to go through with the tattoo. It was something she wanted and was looking forward to.

30

Teal sealed the envelope. Another letter to send off to Dottie. So far, she had sent four and Dottie had replied twice.

She had actually been surprised that Dottie had written back. It was comforting. It was nice getting real mail for a change. Dottie promised her she would soon send pictures of where she lived, the beautiful Braga, Portugal. Dottie had noticed Teal's interest when she mentioned the pastry shops and churches with their pretty mosaics on the walls and had suggested it herself.

Teal couldn't wait to see the pictures. She'd already looked stuff up on the Internet, but of course, the pictures wouldn't be the same.

A message came through from Olive.

> Can I borrow $25 just until next week?-O
>
> For what?-T

Normally, Teal wouldn't have asked what Olive needed the money for, but the last thing she wanted was to hand over money to Olive so she could buy alcohol. Although Olive might not have been an alcoholic, the fact that she had shown up with the smell of alcohol on her breath at the funeral was worrisome. Teal had reservations so that was enough to justify asking Olive why she needed the money.

> I just need a few things.-O
>
> All right. Are you going to come and pick it up?-T
>
> Yeah. If that works for you?-O
>
> Okay. Sounds good.-T

***

An hour later, Olive showed up to collect the money. Together, they sat on Teal's bed and made small talk.

Apparently, not a lot was new with either of them. Or so it seemed.

Teal could tell her about Jackson but didn't want to. Their relationship was still new so the last thing she needed was having Olive try to make things work between the two of them, or something else. Teal was on her own this time and for once, she preferred it this way.

"Looks like I might be part of my dad's wedding. It's still at least a few months away but lots to do. Kind of exciting. Especially since Tonya is letting me pick out my dress and everything. Toby is going to wear something to match with me and we'll walk down the aisle together. It'll be so cute. You should come. I'm sure they wouldn't mind."

Teal tried small talk. She really was at a loss for words. It seemed like the two of them had grown apart.

***

Later that night at the supper table, Teal noticed that her mother seemed preoccupied. She figured it was none of her business. If her mother wanted to talk about it, she would. It wasn't like her mother was shy or anything.

She did wonder, though, if she was going to mention the private detective she'd hired to spy on her father and Tonya. Maybe she already had some dirt on them.

It seemed exciting for thirty seconds, and then Teal realized this was her life, and well, maybe she really didn't want to know. She had a lot on her mind already. There was Jackson, Olive, the upcoming wedding and still adjusting to the fact that Miss Tate was really gone.

"It was nice of Olive to stop in and visit. But she didn't stay very long. Did she have somewhere to be?"

There it was. Her mother wanted to know why Olive had been over and why she'd left so quickly.

Teal was slightly annoyed. It shouldn't matter to her mother when her friends stopped by and how long they stayed.

Within reason of course. She didn't want to admit it to herself, but she had been disappointed that Olive wasn't able to spare more than ten minutes out of her "busy schedule" to visit. That's probably what annoyed her the most, as opposed to the question she had just been asked.

"Yeah she stopped by for a bit but couldn't stay long."

"Ah. How come she could didn't stay to hang out for a bit?"

She knew better. Her mother wouldn't have asked these questions without a reason. Suddenly her mind flashed back to when her mother had asked about Brad dating Olive and how she had seen Brad with Trina and what not. This was not a good sign. Something was definitely up.

"She said she had to go pick up a few things," Teal replied.

"So she came all the way over here to tell you she couldn't hang out because she had to go pick up some things. That doesn't make much sense."

Looks like her mother knew it was more than that. Damn it. There was no way out of it. It was time to fess up about the money.

"Actually, she asked to borrow twenty-five dollars until next week. After she got it, she headed out." There. It was out. She had admitted she had lent Olive money.

Her mother's head went back and forth. "I guess that means Olive's mom refused to give her any."

"Why would she say no? Olive's always good at paying back what she borrows. Are they fighting or something?" This scene wasn't making sense. Like a lot of other things that had happened lately.

Teal couldn't put her finger on it, but something wasn't right. She had missed a detail somewhere. No matter, it would just be a few minutes most likely before her mother would tell her what that detail was.

"Olive's mother probably knew what she was going to use the money for and didn't agree with it, so refused to give her any." This, Teal's mother informed her with raised eyebrows.

"Was it for alcohol? Please tell me it wasn't for that." Teal hoped she was right. The last thing she needed to know was that she was the one who had inadvertently provided alcohol to Olive.

"No, not alcohol. I know Olive has been drinking here and there but so far, it doesn't seem to be a problem. At the moment the problem is Brad."

Teal shoved the last piece of the pizza into her mouth and took extra long chewing it to give her time to figure out what to say next. She wasn't about to argue with her mother, but at the same time, she needed to know what was going on.

What did Brad have to do with her loaning Olive money? Unless Brad had asked Olive to get money for something he needed. But that didn't make sense either because there was no way Olive would approach her mother to ask for money to help out Brad.

"Are you saying that Brad asked her to get him money?" She knew she couldn't hide the disbelief in her eyes. If this was the case, they were back together. Not good.

"No, I don't think he asked her to get money. I think she took it upon herself. I'm guessing she wants to put the money into his account for the canteen. You know. So he can grab chips, chocolate bars and other things like that."

Teal shook her head. What was Brad doing at a

canteen? No way would he work at a job like that. He wasn't any good at dealing with the public, he had zero patience. It would be only a matter of time before he was fired. It was a good thing her mother had hired a private detective to find out information because *Teal* sure as heck wasn't any good at finding stuff out. Not even from her best friend.

"I don't think Brad works at a canteen, Mom." She raised her eyebrows at her mother. She rose, picked up her plate, rinsed it and placed it in the sink. At least, for once, she could give her mother some information instead of the other way around. This was good because she always felt silly when she found out information about her own friends from her own mother. It wasn't supposed to be like that. Not when it came to your friends.

"You haven't heard? Are you serious? Olive didn't tell you?"

Teal stared at her mother and waited. Another shoe was about to be dropped.

"I heard it from Olive's mother, so it is true,. Word has also gotten around. Gossip usually does. Remember the incident a few days ago with Brad trying to break into Olive's house? As you know, he was arrested. Normally, the police would have kept him inside for a night or two and then released him on bail. However, when they got Brad to the police station and ran his name—standard procedure—they found out there was a bench warrant out for failure to appear in court. That charge was from when he was arrested a few months back for assault. He'd been in a fight with some guy."

Teal sat back down in her chair. How could she not have known? She wanted to smack Olive right now. Her best friend hadn't told her what was going on? Olive may not have known months ago that Brad had gotten mixed up in something, but since she knew enough to get money for him now, she had to know why he hadn't been released on bail. Teal couldn't believe this was happening. She waited for her mother to continue.

"So they currently have him up at the Innes jail. He's eighteen so that's where he goes. He isn't sure yet how long he's going to be there. There's a good chance he'll be out in a couple of weeks, most likely on bail. That's because there's so much overcrowding. I heard that some of the newer inmates coming in have to sleep on the floor until someone else is released. Like I said, I'm sure Olive borrowed the money from you to put in his canteen at the jail. That way he can have access to cookies and stuff. I heard that one of the things inmates do to pass the time is place bets on different fights and other drama that's going on in the jail. In jail, one of the currencies is digestive cookies that you can only get from the canteen." Her mother giggled.

Although it wasn't all that funny, Teal found herself smiling, too. "Seriously? That's what they use?" She knew this wasn't a joke, but it was pretty funny to think of Brad in jail, placing bets on fights using cookies.

If Olive had gone this far, to not mention that Brad was in jail and that she needed to borrow money to put in his canteen, it confirmed what she knew. Brad and Olive were definitely back together.

Teal inhaled deeply. She needed to let go. Olive was

old enough to make her own decisions. If Olive was dealing with Brad, that meant that Teal wouldn't have to deal with Olive. She hoped the incident on the Ferris wheel would remain buried.

Her mother continued. "Teal, honey. I know you've been trying to figure out what I've been up to on the computer and why I've been going out more than usual and what not. I guess it's best that I tell you what's going on before you come up with your own conclusions and probably be way off base."

"Okay. Sounds good. Tell me." She waited without breathing.

"Let me say first that I am not seeing anyone. Since your father left, things have been rather quiet which means I have more time on my hands. It can get lonely. So I decided to find something to keep me busy. I'm taking a course. An online course."

"Like a college or university credit or something?"

"Nothing like that. Not even close." Her mother smiled. "I came across a course on how to become a private investigator."

Teal covered her mouth with her hand.

"Don't laugh. It seemed really interesting, so I looked into it more and registered a couple months ago. I've been spending a lot of time on it. In fact, I am now working on the last few requirements leading up to my final exam." Her mother waited for a response.

Teal folded her arms across her chest and bit her tongue to buy some time. Wasn't this just a kick in the pants? No way would she tell her mother what she thought she had been up to. So as it turned out her mother hadn't hired somebody to spy on Teal's father, she was doing homework assignments. Teal struggled to keep the laughter in, because, if she let it out, her mother would think it was directed at her. Definitely not the case. What in the world had she been thinking?

As she rose from her chair to go to her room, she stopped to pat her mother on the shoulder. "I think it's great that you are finally getting the chance to do the things you want to do. Let me know if there's anything I can do to help. If you need me to practice with you or to study, we can do that as well."

"That's sweet of you, Teal. Your support means a lot to me."

31

TEAL COULDN'T HELP HOW SHE FELT. She had been betrayed. Olive knew that if she had told Teal what she wanted the money for, Teal would not have lent it to her. And Olive would have been right because Teal would not have done so. Not to help Brad out.

It was Brad's own fault he was in jail and especially so since he had been arrested more than once, then had skipped out on his court date, and continued to act like nothing had happened. No. He had to own up to his mistakes and Teal was not about to help him either directly or indirectly. It was now time for him to pay the piper. She had heard this very same expression from Miss Tate.

And furthermore, no matter what happened, there was no way she would hang out with Brad and Olive. No way.

Nor would she let Olive rope her into trying to save

Brad or anything like that. If Olive wanted to rescue him, all the power to her. There was no way Teal would be a part of it, no matter what. She couldn't trust Olive anymore.

A text from Jackson came through on Teal's cell phone.

> I'm nervous about tomorrow.-J
>
> Me too. No worries, though. My mom is really chill. So is my dad. And Tonya and Toby, too. But I don't want to scare you away just yet so we'll start with just Mom for now. lol-T
>
> I can't wait to see you tomorrow.-J
>
> Same.-T

***

Teal was happy that she didn't have to go through formally meeting Jackson's mother like Jackson was going to be doing with her family. Teal already knew Jackson's mom from school. That made things easier. They had never had an issue with each other, so hopefully it would stay that way.

Teal wanted to introduce Jackson to her father, Tonya and even Toby, but not right now. She wanted to see how things would be going in a couple of months. Who knew, maybe she would wake up tomorrow and the time with Jackson would have been nothing but a dream. Teal hoped it wasn't a dream.

The two of them hadn't really sat down and had The Talk, as they say on the Internet sites for relationships, but she was pretty sure they were dating. Not that she would ever admit to anyone else that she'd been spending several hours a day on different sites checking out message boards and analyzing everything Jackson said to find out what it truly meant. She would feel silly if anyone found out.

Teal tried to work up the nerve to ask him. She was too embarrassed to do it in person, face to face. She had thought of sending him a text. It might be lame, but so far so good and although they did talk on the phone often, both of them were comfortable sending messages back and forth. It just worked better for the two of them.

Her mother suggested it might be best if they ordered in something when Jackson came over for supper the next day.

Teal agreed that they could each order something they liked.

Jackson didn't have any allergies. She'd already asked.

Surprisingly, she was the one who had brought it up to her mother, about Jackson coming for supper, so they could meet. Her mother seemed caught off guard but looked happy about it. Definitely a good sign.

Considering all the lectures she used to get about dating when she talked about Olive, she was surprised her mother hadn't freaked out. Maybe her mother was starting to mellow out?

Teal spotted the envelope on the bed. It was a letter from Dottie. She pushed it aside to read later.

She was happy that they had kept in touch. She had told Dottie about Jackson and also about her mother's hiring a private detective. She had asked for Dottie's thoughts on whether she should give her father a heads-up or not and could barely wait to find out Dottie's opinion. Not that it mattered anymore since her mother had told her what she'd been up to. Still, Dottie's letters were always interesting.

32

Teal's mother shook Jackson's hand when Teal introduced them. This was a good sign.

They decided to order in from Milano, a pizza place a few blocks down the street. Their specialty was pizza but they offered a little bit of everything on their menu.

Her mother decided on a veggie sub, Jackson on a hero sub and Teal ordered a small poutine.

Now that Jackson was there, she was a lot more nervous than she thought she would be. No way would she admit it to her mother, though. If she got hungry later, she'd find something else in the house to snack on.

As soon as they sat down to eat, her mother started in with the questions. "You're finishing high school this year. Do you know what you want to do when you're done? Do you plan on going to college? Or university? Or are you taking time off first?" At least her mother had waited until they were sitting down.

It looked like Jackson had come up with the same strategy Teal herself used when she needed to stall for more time to answer a question: take an extra big bite of something and take your time chewing it. Yes. He was definitely her type of guy.

"I'm probably going to college or university right after high school. I don't want to lose time, as they say. I am most likely going to go into computers. I hear that's the way things are going these days and Dad always said I should go into it because I was particularly good at it. I would kind of like to do it for him as well as for me, you know? In honor of his memory." Jackson picked up the second half of his sub.

Teal smiled inside. What a sweetheart. Jackson gave all the right answers and the two of them hadn't even practiced or anything. There was no way her mother would be able to come up with a list of faults.

"Sounds like you have things figured out. That's good. And actually, that's great about doing it for your father, but make sure this is something *you* really want as well. It's good that you admire him so much, but don't forget you're your own person."

"I know. I really do like computers though."

Teal felt like she was floating on air. Things were going ten times better than she could ever have imagined. Until she accidentally knocked over Piper's water bowl while grabbing a bottle of water for Jackson and her from the fridge, that is.

Both socks were wet now. The left sock soaked right through. She grabbed paper towels from the roll and dabbed at the floor then sat back on her chair.

Jackson and Teal laughed at this and Teal was happy to realize this broke the nervousness that had been surrounding them over supper.

Teal removed her right sock first. Then the left sock. Oh, no. She immediately tucked that foot behind the other to hide her new tattoo.

Too late. Her mother had spotted it. "What the hell is that?"

This wasn't good.

Jackson froze in his seat and Teal knew why. If the true story unfolded while he was there, he would be dead for sure and he knew it. It wouldn't matter how much her mother had liked him and what an awesome impression he had made. If her mother knew he had played a part in Teal's tattoo, it was game over. For the both of them.

Her mother leaned down and actually grabbed Teal's foot to take a closer look.

It was obvious Jackson didn't know what to do. Not that she could blame him. He had even moved his chair further away as if to put more space between an angry mother and her daughter.

"This had better be fake and some sort of joke. I'm telling you. It had better be."

Teal watched in horror as her mother licked her thumb and tried rubbing at the tattoo. As if by rubbing it she would be able to get rid of it, as though Teal had drawn it on in marker or something.

Teal couldn't handle the embarrassment. She covered her eyes, hoping if she kept her hands there long enough, everything would go away by itself.

"Mom! Stop it!"

Jackson stood up. He stuffed his hands into his pockets, removed them, then stuffed them in again.

Teal turned to him with tears in her eyes. "What say maybe you should go home for now and we can chat later?"

Her mother let go of her foot. "Teal's right. I think it's time for you to go. It was nice meeting you and hopefully we'll see you again. Go say your goodbye, Teal." Her mother turned her back on her.

Teal walked Jackson to the door. She was at a loss for words.

"I hope things aren't too rough with your mom. Are you going to be okay alone here?" Jackson edged closer to her.

"Yeah. It'll be fine. I mean, it's not going to be easy, but Mom's never hit me or anything. Although I've never been in this much trouble before."

"I guess if I don't hear from my girlfriend for a while it will be because your phone will be taken away?" Jackson grinned.

She didn't move. Had he just said what she thought he'd said? That she was his *girlfriend*? This was awesome. Except for the fact that she may never be allowed out of the house again to see said "boyfriend." At least she could now say she had a boyfriend. This was a good start.

"I'm your girlfriend?" she asked quietly.

"If you want to be." Jackson raised his eyebrows in a question.

"Yes." She leaned in and kissed him.

***

Jackson was gone. She was alone with her mother. She had been so excited with the news from Jackson that they were officially an item, she had nearly forgotten about the tattoo and the fallout that surely awaited her.

33

Teal walked into the living room where her mother was sitting on the couch and sat on a chair with Piper and waited for her mother to speak. She didn't know what to say because she had a feeling that no matter what she said, her mother was still going to be pissed off.

"Teal, I can't believe what you did. It was so stupid. I can't even talk to you right now. Just go to your room and we'll talk later when I've had time to think. And breathe." Her mother pointed in the direction of Teal's bedroom and then walked away.

Teal still had her phone for now so that was good. She would be able to keep in touch with Jackson. Honestly though, she just wanted to get things over with, especially the punishment, whatever that might be. The not knowing would be the worst and was already starting to drive her crazy and she'd only been in her room for a few minutes.

Dottie's letter was still on the bed. She picked it up. Strange. It was heavier than usual. Maybe Dottie had included pictures with the letter. She moved her fingers around the envelope to feel around. Strange, it didn't feel like pictures. She detected an outline of something small and firm.

As she opened the envelope, a small metal key fell out. She picked it up. The letter was definitely from Dottie.

She picked it up and read.

Dear Teal,

It was good to hear from you. I'm glad we're still writing to each other. This letter will be short because it's important and I want to post it in this morning's mail.

First of all, I wouldn't feel comfortable telling you what to do about your mother hiring someone to check up on your father. If that's what happened. That decision is yours and yours alone to make. I would write out the good and the bad about telling him, and then make your decision from there.

As you have probably noticed, there's a metal key inside the envelope with this letter. It's yours. It's from Miss Tate. Several months ago, she asked me to hold onto it until after she was gone and then send it to you. Your mother knows about the key but had told me not to mention it. To just send it when the time was right. Now that you have the key, let your mother know. She'll tell you about it.

Waiting to hear back. I hope all is well.

Your friend,

Dottie

Teal didn't know what to do. What was the key was for? No, cross that out. Would she be able to approach her mother right now? About anything? Even about the key?

She decided to wait it out and write in her journal.

After she had filled several pages, a glance at her cell phone told her an hour had passed. Had her mother calmed down any? She would take her chances.

"Mom, I know you're upset with me, but I got a letter from Dottie today. It has a key with it. She told me to ask you about it."

Teal decided not to sit in case she needed to make a run for her room.

"It's for your safety deposit box at the bank."

"My what?" A safety deposit box? What was her mother talking about?

"I'll arrange for an appointment for the day after tomorrow. Good night."

Not a good sign.

***

As they arrived at the bank, Teal grabbed her mother's hand. "Can we just stand outside the bank for a moment?"

"Of course. Take all the time in the world. We can take as long as we need. We don't even have to do it today. We can even come back another time if you like."

Her mother seemed as nervous as Teal was.

They stood there outside Scotia Bank, not speaking, not moving while the box waited for them.

"Do you know what's in it?" Teal asked.

"Not a clue. I think I'm as excited as you are."

That's good to hear, Teal thought. She doesn't sound angry anymore. Progress. She would take it.

Her right hand shook as she put the key into the box. It took two tries but finally the metal box opened. They stared at each other.

"Teal, honey. There's nothing to worry about. She left you a little something of value. Obviously. Or why would she have put it in a safety deposit box? That's my thinking anyway." Her mother shrugged.

Her mother had a point. What her mother said made sense. Her mother had been executor of the will, but Dottie claimed that the contents of this particular safety deposit box belonged to Teal. That's all. Just the word "contents," not what those contents might be.

Teal dumped the box over and she could feel her eyes widen as wide as they'd ever widened. Money. Cash. Cold hard cash, as they say in the movies. There were pictures and a letter from Miss Tate.

Her mother clapped her hands. "Oh, Teal. Look!"

Teal was excited but at the same time in the back of her mind, she hoped this would take her mother's mind off the whole tattoo situation. Perhaps she wouldn't be grounded until after prom next year after all.

Teal quickly scanned the letter which stated that Miss Tate had left her money for college and enough to take her to a place she wanted her to visit, by plane! It looked like sometime in the next while she would get to visit Dottie in Spain.

Her mother moved in behind her to read the letter over her shoulder. "Are you spoiled or what?"

"Definitely spoiled."

"And don't think I've forgotten about the tattoo."

It felt to Teal that her whole body sagged. Of course it had been wishful thinking on her part, but yeah, she knew she'd have to pay something for getting that tattoo.

"What's the punishment?" she asked as she tucked everything but Miss Tate's letter back into the safety deposit box. She didn't want to turn and look at her mother.

"No phone for a month. You can hand it over tomorrow. That gives you enough time to explain to your friends why you will be off line." Her mother actually shook her finger at Teal. "And if you ever pull a stunt like that again, you can go live at your father's or somewhere else for that matter. I will not put up with that kind of crap."

Teal turned now to look at her mother, waiting for the rest of her punishment to be meted out. Was there more to come?

"Got it?"

"Yes. Definitely."

***

Things hadn't turned out so bad after all. She still had Jackson. Her mother wasn't trying to sabotage her father.

Her father was getting married. Teal would be getting a baby brother, Toby. Although Miss Tate was gone, she had Dottie, and Miss Tate had left her money to help pay for at least the first year of college. She hadn't counted the money. She had no phone but would still be able to leave the house, at least.

The only thing that was truly still up in the air was her friendship with Olive. Teal sighed. There wasn't much she could do about *that* one. Either things would work out between them or they wouldn't. The best she could do was take things one day at a time and be willing to listen if Olive came to her senses.

This Is It

34

Teal couldn't believe it had been only a week since her father and Tonya's wedding and that things were finally getting back to normal. But now that all the hype was over, life seemed a tad on the dull side.

The wedding had gone off without a hitch. Bonus. Toby had walked down the aisle with Teal and the crowd had gone wild over how adorable he was all dressed up in his cute tuxedo. The wedding photos weren't as nerve racking as Teal had thought they would be, either. Another bonus. But there had been no honeymoon plans for the newlyweds. When Teal had inquired why, her father had told her it was because neither he nor Tonya had been able to get time off work, but the main thing was, they were still dealing with the final papers for Toby's adoption.

At least there was still Christmas to look forward to. Teal would have time with the family before worrying too much about applying for college and university. She'd spent the last couple of months pouring over catalogs, talking with her mother and father about her choices, and even with Jackson. Everyone had been supportive. In the end, though, it was Teal who had to decide what she wanted to do.

Jackson was now attending Algonquin College. He was in his first year, in a general computers course, and had one more exam to do before he was officially finished his first semester. Teal was proud of him. She had to admit it made her feel quite mature to be dating someone who was in college when she herself was in high school, even if it was her last year.

Then there was the cost for college and university. The application fee alone was over a hundred dollars. And that fee was to apply to *either* college or university, not both. Nowadays, it seemed there was a fee for—in her mother's words—"every damned thing." Both her mother and father had some money put aside for her, and Teal was glad for that as she didn't think she could handle going to school full time and working a ton of hours on top of that. School had to be her top priority. She did not want to mess it up. There were so many things at stake. Maybe it was best that she put the whole college business out of her mind until after the Christmas holidays were over? Weren't the holidays stressful enough without adding anything to them? What about university? Should she try to get into that first, and then college could be her plan B? Like, if university didn't accept her, maybe she could go to college? What was the difference between the two? Heck, maybe she should consider taking a year off school. That idea sounded nice, but she knew that neither of her parents would ever let her do such a thing. She shook her head. She *had* to let this stuff go until the New Year.

"Okay, Toby. I'm ready!"

Three seconds later, Toby was running full speed into the kitchen, just as she'd expected. In fact, she would have been disappointed if he hadn't. He was, after all, officially her step-brother now that her father and his mother were married. Teal even had a small picture of "her little brother" that she carried around in her wallet. The picture had been taken at the park. She'd snapped it there when she babysat him once. In the picture, he sat in the sand, playing with cars and smiling up at the camera.

"Yay! Yummy." His eyes widened at the supplies he saw laid out before him: all the necessary ingredients for making a gingerbread house. Slabs of ginger, gummy bears, gumdrops, vanilla icing, chocolate icing, and gingerbread people. Teal had been looking forward to this. Now, she just needed to make sure Toby did not stuff most of the candy into his mouth while they made the actual house or else he'd be up all night running around in circles and she'd be the one who'd have to put him to bed. She was not feeling up to bedtime duty tonight.

She remembered one of the times she'd babysat. Toby had kept asking for more candy and squealed with delight each time she handed him a piece, so she'd continued giving him more. It was fun at first. One minute, he was clapping his hands and was happy and the next minute, he had puked all over the kitchen floor. The spew had gone everywhere. It had been so gross, Teal had nearly vomited when she attempted to clean up the mess. Of course, the whole time she was busy doing that, Toby was running around the house asking for more candy. Not only did she have to clean it all up, she had tried hard to keep the whole thing from her father's and Tonya's notice. She did not want them to think she'd been irresponsible.

Lucky for her, Toby had just thrown up the once and they had spent the rest of the afternoon reading books and watching a movie, although just fifteen minutes into the movie he fell asleep on her lap. That was when she knew she loved the little sweetheart.

At supper that night, he did not eat as much as usual, but enough that Tonya and Teal's father had not suspected anything and the whole babysit-candy-puke episode was still unknown to them. Teal hoped to keep it that way. Lesson learned. She would not let that happen again on her watch.

35

IT DEFINITELY FELT DIFFERENT having a little kid around during the Christmas holidays. It made the whole holiday experience a lot more special and Teal enjoyed the season even more now that Toby and Tonya were around to share it with.

This year, it had been decided Toby would play the role of "Santa" and give out the presents to each person. That was fine with Teal. It was not like she was a kid anymore. She could wait to open her presents. All she had really hinted at, present-wise, was for a stereo and a gift card to the stationery store that Tonya had taken her to before. That way, she could pick out her own journals. Since Teal's wish list was never very long, more often than not, she got what she wanted for Christmas.

Teal saw Tonya give her father's leg a squeeze. After that, Tonya gave a gift box about the size of her father's hand to Toby.

"This present is for Teal. Take it to her, Toby, so she can open it."

"Pes-ant for Tee! Pes-ant for Tee!" Toby squealed. He sat down right in front of her and clapped his hands. "Ready? Open!" He clapped his hands once again.

This was the first present of hers to open. She was definitely curious to see what it was. It was not the stereo for sure. It might be the gift card. Dad usually put gift cards inside a card or something. He had never taken the time to put them in an actual box and wrap it or anything. She doubted he had changed his gift-wrapping techniques this late in the game.

Teal took off the wrapping paper. The box was generic with nothing on it to give away any hints about what might be inside. She lifted the lid slowly. Inside was something covered in white tissue paper. By now, Toby was nearly sitting on top of her as he watched and waited to see what was inside the box. Teal picked up the item and carefully unwrapped the tissue paper. Usually, when she received stuff covered in tissue paper, it was fragile.

Her father said, "I think it might be upside down. You might have to flip it over. But carefully."

No longer puzzled, Teal looked at him. That meant the item was breakable. Interesting for sure.

It looked like a picture frame. Why would they give her a picture frame? She turned it over.

"Now?" Toby asked, looking over at his mother.

"Yes. You can tell her." Tonya said smiling.

"Baaaaaabbby!" Toby clasped his hands together.

Toby said it just as Teal flipped the picture frame

over. It took a moment, but then she realized what Toby meant. Inside the picture frame was a black and white photo with the outline of a baby. In her hand, she was holding an ultrasound picture. Teal seriously did not know what to say. This had been the last thing she had expected. Adopting Toby, okay. Her father getting married, okay. It had never even occurred to her that her father and Tonya might have a child together.

"Are you serious? It's ours? The baby… is ours?" Teal wasn't sure how else to put it. She was excited but was overwhelmed at the same time.

"Yes, the baby is ours." Tonya exclaimed, beaming at Teal's father.

Teal rose from her seat. It seemed appropriate to hug Tonya first, so she did, then she hugged her father. She congratulated them.

As she sat down on the floor, Toby walked over to her. "Budder. Budder. Budder," Toby repeated. He was going to be a brother.

Teal gave him a high-five. "Yes, you are going to be a big brother!"

Teal could not believe it.

She turned to her father and Tonya who looked so happy together, and now they were adding one more to the family.

It was only after Toby mentioned he was going to be a brother that she realized she was going to be a sister. She would have another sibling. She'd always wanted a brother or sister. She had Toby now, of course, but with this next one, she would be there from the very start.

At that, Toby decided handing out that one gift had

been enough for him. He was more interested in opening his own presents. While he did that, Teal decided to get more information. Everyone seemed to be in good spirits, so no time like now. She wanted to know everything, right from the very beginning.

"When is the baby due? Do we know yet?"

"In about six months," her father answered.

"Oh my gosh. Is it a boy or a girl? Do we know?" Suddenly, it seemed like the only important thing was the sex of the baby. Not that it should matter, but right at this moment it did.

Tonya took this question. "They believe we are having a girl."

Teal surprised herself when she actually clapped her hands, just as Toby did when he got excited. It would be awesome. Teal already had a brother, and now she would have a baby sister.

For Christmas, Teal's mother gave her a few smaller things like bath bombs, candles and hand cream along with money for her trip. Without a doubt, this had been the best Christmas she could ever have. No way had she thought this would be possible after seeing her parents split up.

Here she was, though, enjoying Christmas with her parents. Separately, but still, they both seemed genuinely happy, and Teal felt happier than she had in a long time. It felt great.

36

Teal noticed that her mother had quickly shut the binder in her hands as soon as Teal entered the living room. Her mother had not been spending as much time on the computer, but had been going out a lot more for short intervals "just to grab a coffee." That seemed suspicious. Her mother had never done that before. Teal started wondering if maybe her mother was finally dating someone, and meeting that person at a coffee shop away from the apartment so there would be no chance Teal would run into him or her. That was smart. Wait and see how things go for a while before letting Teal meet the person. Very responsible of her.

"Let me guess. You're going out to grab a coffee."

Her mother put the binder and a few other items into a laptop bag. "I will be back in a couple of hours. I left money for you and Jackson to order in pizza. I would prefer you stay in tonight."

"We plan to stay in and I am not getting another tattoo anytime soon, Mom. I promise." Teal raised her eyebrows. She figured a decade from now, her mother would still be bringing up the tattoo incident.

***

After Jackson and Teal had eaten, Teal searched through her backpack to find what she was looking for: a couple of items she'd found in the lock box at the bank.

"Ah. You're finally going to tell me what the box was." Jackson smiled at her.

"I still don't believe it myself. I can't believe Miss Tate left it to me."

Teal showed him a photograph of a quaint house situated among others similar in shape, size and color. It appeared to be in a village with old cobblestone-type streets. Already, Teal was enchanted and she hadn't laid eyes on it in reality.

"This is yours?"

"Yep. There are a couple of conditions placed on it, but they're simple. I have to visit the place at least three times and I can't sell it for three years. It doesn't matter how long my visit is, I just have to physically visit it three times. After that, I can do whatever I want with it."

Teal was excited. The house was all hers. She had no idea if she would sell the place, rent it out, or what, but it seemed exciting that those decisions were ultimately hers to make.

"Sounds great, Teal. But are you going to be able to go visit? Or stay there? I don't mean to make you do a reality check, but the cost of airfare will probably be at least a grand. Doing that three times, plus the money you'll need when you go grocery shopping and that kind of thing. And you have college coming up. Wow. A lot of expenses." Jackson raised his eyebrows in a silent question.

Teal stood quietly.

"I'm just saying you may not be able to visit this year."

"Well, I plan on going after graduation. For a month." Teal couldn't help but let out a small squeal after actually saying this. It was exciting just thinking about taking her first plane ride, and to Spain, and to stay in her own house!

"Sounds like a good plan, getting a visit in before college or university starts, but are you going to be able to pay for it?" Doubt was obvious on Jackson's face.

Teal couldn't wait to tell Jackson. The house was not the only thing Miss Tate had left her.

"Miss Tate left me money, too. She wanted to make sure I would be able to go visit the house without worrying about paying for the airfare. Good thing you're sitting down, eh, Jackson? You ready for this? She left me ten thousand dollars!" Teal jumped up and down; she was still shocked by the news herself.

"You have to be joking. Why would she leave you money? And a house? You guys weren't even related or anything. She only knew you a couple years."

Teal folded her arms across her chest. Jealous. That was it. He was jealous of the money. He couldn't care less about the house, but the money bothered him.

"I called Dottie after we opened the box at the bank.

Apparently, Miss Tate had money. She never married, or had kids. She worked until she was sixty-five and she invested her money here and there. Miss Tate started putting money away when she got her first job at the age of fourteen, delivering newspapers. I'm not sure of the exact amount, but she had nearly half a million dollars. She left me what I told you and the rest went to Dottie."

"That's crazy. Good she had money put away, though. She didn't have to worry about becoming one of those cat ladies who also ends up eating wet cat food out of the cans because they don't have enough money to buy proper food." Jackson touched her hand.

"I don't get the money all at once. I get five thousand in May this year, and then twenty-five hundred a year later, and the last chunk a year after that. According to Dottie, Miss Tate figured, with the five thousand she gave me this year, I would be able to spend a couple of weeks at my place in Spain—listen to me, *my* place—and the rest of the money would help pay my tuition for my first semester of school."

"For a grumpy old lady, she sure was smart and turned out to be a pretty amazing person. Lucky you."

Teal still wasn't sure by his tone if he was excited for her or not.

"Definitely an amazing lady," she said. "I wish she was still around so I could visit. I know an elderly man moved into her apartment. I think he's alone. Except for a cat, speaking of cats."

This made Jackson smile.

"I saw him walking down the hallway. He was wearing one slipper, the other one was in his hand, and he was using it trying to shoo his cat back into the apartment. I think the cat's name is Oscar. The man has waved to me a few times and I've waved back. I don't know his name yet. Just the cat's name. That's the extent of it."

"For now," Jackson teased.

Teal slapped his leg playfully. She should try to find out the old man's name though.

In a way, she wanted to invite Jackson to go with her on the trip. It would be awesome. Just the two of them on a grand adventure. On the other hand, though, she wanted to make this journey by herself. It almost seemed like a rite of passage or something. In the back of her mind, she was afraid her mother might try to tag along without her knowing. Maybe her mother would arrive in Spain the day after Teal did, say it was only a coincidence she was staying just three blocks from where Teal's house was. Or something like that. She could definitely see her mother attempting to keep her under observation.

Teal decided she needed to remain on her best behavior—within reason of course—until she left for the trip. The last thing she wanted to do was give her mother even one single reason why she couldn't be trusted. This would take some effort. Teal hoped she was up to the challenge.

37

It had been a quiet Saturday. Just when Teal decided to curl up to write in her journal, her phone went off.

A message from Olive.

> Hey, Teal, just wondering what you're up to?-O

Teal smiled. She knew Olive better than that. Olive never sent a message to ask what she was doing. What Olive really meant was "Are you doing anything important because I need you for something."

Teal debated.

She was comfortable and didn't want to move. The last couple of days had been great, but they'd tired her out. All the Christmas stuff had been fun, but now she wanted to rest. She wanted to write down some of those good memories to hold onto until a time came when things might not be going so great.

> Nothing, was just about to write in my

> journal. You?-T

Teal should at least see what her friend had to say before she made any decisions.

> I'm in trouble.-O

Teal sat up straight. Olive rarely admitted it when things were about to hit the fan, and she *never* did right from the beginning. This was completely out of character for her. Definitely not a good sign.

Teal typed quickly.

> Where are you? Are you safe? Are you okay? What's going on?-T

This brought back memories of the time Teal had to go over to Olive's house because Brad, Olive's ex, was trying to break in.

It was probably only a second or two until the screen indicated Olive was typing back, but it felt a lot longer than that.

> Calm down, Teal. I'm safe. I promise I'm safe. I'm at home. Mom is gone out and no one is here. Just me.

> I need you to come over. Can you do that?-O

This was weird. How could Olive be in trouble if she was safe at home? No one else was in the house. She had not been attacked or anything. Olive had never lied to her before. Olive had left things out, yes, but she had not lied up front. Therefore, this probably was not some sort of prank. Olive truly did seem upset.

> When do you want me to come over?-T

> As soon as you can. Like, right now would be great.-O
>
> Okay, on my way.-T

Teal shut the journal and put it away. Her phone beeped again.

> Thanks, Teal.-O

She stared at the phone for a full ten seconds. This was not like Olive. It wasn't in her character. Olive rarely said thanks. It wasn't her style.

***

Teal was getting frustrated. She'd been at Olive's house for quite a while now and still had no idea why Olive wanted her there.

Olive paced the room. Every so often, she would glance over at Teal, but did not say a word. Finally, Olive tossed a small package at her.

Teal caught it and sat on the bed. She turned the package over to read the English side of it. This was indeed mega serious.

"Oh my god. Seriously?" Teal looked up at Olive.

To her credit, Olive did not look like she was joking and seemed genuinely upset. It looked like she had tears in her eyes. She stopped pacing.

"That's why I wanted you to come over. I wanted someone. Needed someone. Needed *you* to be with me when I did the test." Olive blew her nose with a tissue from a box beside her bed.

Teal's eyes widened. "Did you already read the instructions?" She felt as though she had to tread extra carefully.

"Yep. Pee on the stick and wait for the stripes. One stripe means you are clear and two stripes mean you have something to fear." Olive walked back and forth again.

Teal had to stifle a laugh. She had no idea where Olive had heard that saying but it seemed both appropriate and funny at the same time.

"Okay. I'm going to do it. Give me the stick." Olive took the pregnancy test from Teal and went into the bathroom.

It seemed to take forever, but in fact, Olive had only been gone for about a minute.

Olive hopped onto the bed. "Now we just have to wait for five minutes." Olive set the timer on her cell phone.

"How bad was it going to the store to buy it? Were you embarrassed?" Teal had managed to enter a tattoo studio and have a tattoo, but did not think she would ever be up to the task of walking into a store to buy a pregnancy test.

"As if. I went to the pharmacy at the Rideau mall and guess what. One of Mom's friends, her name's Holly, was working the counter. No way could I do it. And of course I couldn't wait. I lifted it."

Teal stared at her. What was she talking about? What did she mean, "lifted" it? "What do you mean?"

"You know what I mean. I stole it." Olive shrugged her shoulders like it was no big deal.

"That was stupid. If they'd seen you, they would

have arrested you. We're not kids anymore, Olive. If we get into trouble, it's not just a slap on the wrist. We're past that." Teal could not believe what Olive had done.

"I needed to find out. It's not exactly as if I can wait a few weeks or something, right? Anyways, that's over with. I have it. I did the test and now we check." She took in a deep breath.

The timer on Olive's cell chirped.

Olive stood. But did not move.

Teal stayed on the bed.

Olive looked toward the bathroom but stayed where she was.

Teal kept her eyes on Olive and Olive did the same to Teal.

"I can't do it," Olive finally said. "I can't look. You do it. Please? Just look at the test and tell me if there's one stripe or two."

Teal was even more confused now. Olive had had the guts to go into a store and actually steal a pregnancy test, but checking the results of the test was something she wasn't able to do?

Teal couldn't understand why *she* had to be the one to go look at the stupid pee stick. Either way, Olive was going to find out in the next few moments if she was pregnant. Or not. Teal stomped into the bathroom. She wanted this over with, to find out one way or another, so they could move on.

On the counter by the sink lay the pee stick that could change Olive's world and therefore, by default, change Teal's as well. Teal knew that no matter what the stick read, Olive had already drawn her into this.

She hesitated, then inched closer.

The results were clearly displayed. She could see *them*. There were two dark pink lines. Olive's test was positive. Olive was pregnant. Teal was paralyzed with fear. If she felt this way, she could not even begin to imagine how Olive would feel when she learned the test's result.

She exited the bathroom, at first, too stunned to speak.

"Tell me." Olive's demand was a whisper—as if by asking quietly, the answer might be the one she wanted to hear. Or if that were to be the case, perhaps there could be time for the results to turn out differently.

Teal still did not trust herself to speak. So instead, she held up two fingers on her right hand, stared at Olive, and nodded yes. She bit her bottom lip.

"It's positive? I'm pregnant?" Olive's face paled.

"Yes." Teal tried to recover from the shock. It wasn't entirely her issue but because of her friendship with Olive, in a way, it partially was.

Olive threw herself onto the bed from where, in between sobs, she murmured "No, not me. No."

Teal was glad she was not in Olive's shoes. Olive's predicament would take time to figure out a solution for. It wasn't a decision to be made lightly. Whatever choice Olive made now would affect the rest of her life. Getting pregnant was something that scared Teal greatly. Although she and Jackson had been together a while, and got along great, they still had not slept together. Jackson had been patient and she appreciated it. Eventually, they would go all the way, but for now, Teal wasn't ready.

Teal was still a virgin and Jackson respected that.

On Teal's way home, she made a detour that took her a couple of blocks away from her place. Olive had given her the pregnancy test to get rid of. She didn't want her mother to accidentally find it. Olive needed time to figure things out before she told her. There was no way Teal was going to bring it home and dump it in *their* garbage in case *her* mother found it. *Her* mother would instantly jump to conclusions and it would blow up into a fight. The incident with the tattoo was still fresh in her mother's mind. It would be a while before that episode smoothed over. Teal shouldn't have felt anything when she passed by a trash bin, but for some reason, she did. Nothing she could put a finger on. It just felt like she shouldn't do it. But she did. She threw out the positive pregnancy test.

So now, the only thing Teal could do was support Olive in whatever decision Olive made. She did hope that everything would work out okay for her friend. It would take time, but things always seemed to get back on track for Olive.

38

Jackson handed Teal a cutout from a magazine. It was a picture of a tuxedo.

"What do you think? Would this be okay for the prom?" He hadn't gone to his own prom. At that time, they had not been together as a couple very long, so he hadn't bothered to go.

Teal grabbed the cutout. "Looks good," she said as she handed it back.

"We don't have to decide now but we will soon." Jackson raised questioning eyebrows at her.

What was that supposed to mean? They had already discussed it, but still…

Teal was fine with the prom itself. She could handle that. What she wasn't sure of was the part that generally happened *after* prom. She realized it was only natural to lose your virginity eventually and Jackson was her first actual relationship.

Jackson shoved the paper into his back pocket. "Teal. The color. We have to decide on the color soon because when I go and put a hold on the suit, they're going to ask me. If we don't decide soon, I'll end up with whatever's left over so there's a good chance we won't match."

Okay, maybe he hadn't been thinking of their having sex together for the first time. On the other hand, maybe he had and then saw Teal's reaction so responded with this matching color thing.

"Yes, okay. Soon. We'll figure out the color scheme soon. I'm undecided."

Teal was telling him the truth. She was trying to make a choice between purple and turquoise as their color scheme. Too many choices to worry about right now.

She was also unsure of what prom night might hold in store for them after the dance was over.

Jackson and Teal had talked about intimacy in general on several occasions. Jackson wasn't a virgin. In a way, she'd been shocked when she found out, but at the same time, she would have been shocked if he had been. As if that made any sense at all.

About a year before he met Teal, Jackson had dated a girl for a couple of months. One night, after a few too many drinks, they had slept together. It hadn't been her first time, but it had been his. A week later, she had broken it off with him and hadn't said why. According to Jackson, they didn't get along that well to begin with, so it was for the best.

The prom was still a few months away. More time to think of how she felt about Jackson and if she was ready for this next step. But right now, above everything else, she needed to figure out what color of dress she would be wearing.

39

OLIVE'S EYES PLEADED. She needed him right now. They had to figure things out. They had to figure out *the situation* they were currently in together. It was not only her responsibility, but his, too. It was not as though she'd managed to get pregnant on her own or anything. But that was the way he was behaving.

"I'm not lying, Brad. I took the test a couple days ago. It came out positive."

"So. What do you want from me?" Brad spat out the words. "What do you want me to do about it?"

Olive knew he would not be happy with the news but she hadn't pictured the discussion going quite like this.

"I want us to talk about it. It's a decision we have to make together." Olive continued to fold his laundry.

"I think this is your problem. Not mine." He turned away from her.

Olive stopped.

"*We* slept together. *We* got pregnant. Therefore, it is a *we* problem." Surely, he was not so ignorant that he could not see that.

"The way I see it, *you* had sex with someone and got pregnant, so it's a *you* problem." Brad stood with his hands on his hips. He definitely looked upset.

"I didn't have sex with *someone*. I had sex with *you*, Brad. Just you, and deep down you know that. It's yours, Brad. Ignoring this is not going to help." Olive stood her ground and was secretly quite impressed with herself.

He stood quietly for a moment. Then, without warning, he lunged forward to slap her hard across the face. She fell to the floor. Her left cheek felt on fire.

"Liar! Get out now!" he hollered.

She could not believe it. He had hit her. She was stunned. She grabbed her bag and ran out the door.

Olive didn't know where to go. She didn't want to hang around outside in case Brad decided to come after her. She didn't want to be anywhere near him. That was the last thing she wanted and needed right now. There was no way she could go home like this. She was too upset. She needed a few hours to calm down before she even thought of going home. It was too bad she didn't have a cool father like Teal did. She hadn't talked to her own father in years.

Teal. She could go to Teal's. She would beg her not to say anything to anyone. She could handle this. Brad had just been a little upset with her. That's all. It was to be expected. She'd had a few days to process the news of the pregnancy, and this was the first he'd heard of it. Everything would be fine once he'd had time to calm down and think things through. That was all. There really wasn't a choice. She had to wait things out. No big deal really. Right?

She wiped tears away, adjusted her bag and immediately felt more in control. Her best bet was to head for Teal's place. Best not to let Teal know she was on her way in case Teal wasn't home, or was busy. No way could she handle that. Best to show up unannounced and take things from there. She kept her fingers crossed as she walked to Teal's. It felt like everyone was staring at her. She tried to stop her tears, but her system wouldn't listen.

***

Teal heard the knock at their apartment door. She smiled. It was probably Jackson, a surprise visit, which she always welcomed.

Her smile faded away quickly when she saw Olive standing there. Olive was a mess, her hair was sticking out in places and Teal could not even see her face clearly. She could tell her best friend had been crying. Still was, in fact, but trying to cover it up.

Right now, words didn't matter. Teal did the first thing that came to mind. She wrapped her arms around her friend.

"Shhh. It's going to be okay. Whatever it is, it will be okay." Teal held onto her.

Arm across Olive's shoulder, Teal guided her to the couch and sat her down. Teal tried to straighten Olive's hair to get it away from her face, but Olive flinched. It took a couple of tries before Teal realized Olive was hiding something.

"Oh my gosh. Did Brad do that? Did he hit you?" Teal could detect a slight swelling on Olive's face.

"I told him I was pregnant, and he got upset," Olive sobbed. "But he'll calm down, and then we can talk. He'll be more reasonable then."

This time, Olive did not pull back when Teal moved the hair away from her face. Olive's cheek had already started to bruise, and her left eye was swollen.

"I'll be right back. I'll go get some ice to put on that."

As Teal was wrapping the ice cubes in a cloth, she heard the apartment door shut.

"Olive. What happened? Were you robbed?" Teal's mother rushed over.

Teal handed Olive the ice to put on her face before shaking her head, no, to her mother.

Her mother's expression was one of confusion.

Teal kept quiet and hoped someone else would say something. She really had no idea what to say or do right at that moment.

"It was Brad, wasn't it?"

For a moment, it looked like her mother was going to continue, maybe even start with a big lecture on the good-for-nothing Brad, but Teal was grateful that her mother had managed to stop herself. The last thing Olive needed right now was a lecture, especially from her best friend's mother.

Teal and her mother managed to get Olive cleaned up. Olive sipped at a hot apple cider. She had not said much but that was okay.

When Olive's cell phone went off, Teal locked eyes with Olive.

"If it's him, don't answer back," Teal's mom advised. "No matter what he says, don't answer him back."

Olive picked up her cell phone and checked the message. It was from Brad.

> This is your entire fault, Olive. How could you let this happen?-B

Teal expected Olive to answer back the moment her mother left the living room to go to the kitchen, but she didn't. Instead, she turned the phone to silent mode and put it back in her purse.

Olive looked up at Teal as she took the last sip of her cider. "Would it be okay if I spent the night here?" Olive's eyes pleaded.

Teal was caught off guard. It had been quite a while since the two of them had had a sleepover.

"Of course. I'll get Mom to call your place to save you having to." Teal smiled as she sat beside Olive on the couch. "How about we order in Chinese food, as well? That sound good?"

She saw the beginnings of a small smile on Olive's lips. "Chinese food and a sleepover sounds really good right now. Thanks."

They touched hands.

***

It was a quiet evening. Olive and Teal ordered in Chinese food and decided to watch four of the *Scream* movies. Those were among Olive's all-time favorites and Teal didn't mind them. Olive didn't say much, but that was okay. The fact that she ate and let out a small laugh every so often during the first movie was enough. A couple of times, Olive gingerly touched her cheek. It broke Teal's heart to watch this happening, but maybe this incident would be enough for Olive to leave Brad for good.

As the second movie started, Teal got a text message. She figured it might be from Jackson. It wasn't. It was from her mother.

> Just wanted to give you a head's up that I have spoken to Olive's mom about what happened. She has either already called or will be calling the police on Brad.
>
> He was supposed to keep out of trouble because he is still out on bail from when he tried to break into Olive's place.
>
> It will just be a matter of time before Brad is picked up and arrested once again.-M

Teal stared at the phone. She didn't know what to say. She was on her mother's side, of course. Brad hadn't followed the rules, and there were consequences for not following rules. But she didn't want Olive to get upset all over again.

Maybe it would be best for Teal to wait until morning to say anything to her. That way there was at least a chance Olive might get some sleep. If she told her now, they'd both be up all night discussing everything.

***

At the table the next morning, Olive brought up the incident first.

Teal was surprised but grateful as well. It would make things easier.

"I took a look in the mirror and I look like crap." Olive accentuated this by gently touching her cheek. "It's even worse than I looked and felt yesterday."

"That's how it usually goes. When you get hurt, it feels worse for the next couple of days. It should feel better soon. Are you going to go back to him for more?" Teal asked this as she stood up to take the dishes to rinse them off in the sink.

If looks could kill, Teal would be dead right now. Olive looked like she was ready to pounce.

Teal stayed at the sink and took her sweet time rinsing the dishes off.

"Are you saying this is my fault?" Olive asked in a raised voice.

"I didn't say that. What I meant was that he has treated you badly before. He cheated on you. He tried to break into your house. And other stuff. Now he has physically abused you. He slapped you, Olive." Teal turned to look at her friend.

Olive made no comment and Teal could not read her face.

"I didn't want to tell you last night, but your mom knows what happened and called the police. Brad is back in jail and they will not let him out for at least a couple days. Maybe even a week. He'll be in there until some of his charges go to court." Teal inched her way toward Olive.

"I figured as much," Olive said as she helped load the dishes into the dishwasher.

"How did you know?"

Olive's smile was more of a smirk. "Easy. Your mother was too calm about the whole thing. I figured the minute we headed to your room to watch the movies, she'd be on the phone to my mom and it would go from there. I was right. I'm actually surprised that my mom didn't show up to give me trouble for being with him and drag me home. I'm glad she didn't. It was good to spend a nice quiet evening with you. No drama. Just like we used to." Then the tears fell freely.

Teal put her arms around her.

40

Teal looked over at the message on her phone's screen. She was supposed to go over to her father's place later on in the afternoon. Maybe plans had changed or something. The message read:

> It's important. Please call me when you get the chance.-Dad

That did not sound good. She closed her journal and turned down the radio before she dialed his number.

"Dad. I got your message. What is going on?"

"It's Tonya. She's at the hospital. Her water leaked and it's too early for the baby to be born yet." Dad's voice sounded weird.

"Oh my gosh. What does this mean? What can we do?"

Instantly, Teal was on her feet pacing her bedroom, but after two fast turns, she stopped. All she had accomplished was to make herself physically dizzy on top of being dizzy with worry.

"Well, like I said, right now we're at the hospital. They have her comfortable and lying in a bed. I have Toby with me. If you don't have any plans, it would be great if you could come here. We're at the Civic. This is where her doctor delivers out of the obstetrical unit. Just ask at the information desk how to get here. I can't be chasing Toby around and trying to figure out what's going on with Tonya at the same time. Of course, the poor little guy doesn't understand what's going on, so he's getting upset. I'm sure he'd love to see you."

He did not need to plead. Of course, she'd go help. After all, Toby was her step-brother and she would soon have a sister. She had responsibilities now. Besides, this was an emergency, a *family* emergency.

"Of course. I'll be there as fast as I can, Dad. I'll text you when I'm close so you can tell me how to get to the information desk. Hang in there, Dad. Love you."

"Are you sure you don't mind? I did talk to your mother and she's willing to help out as well." He didn't sound convinced.

"I'm on my way, Dad." She hung up the phone. She said goodbye to Olive as she left for the hospital.

***

As Teal entered the hospital room, she stopped for a moment. Toby was sitting beside Tonya on the right side of the bed, and was holding her hand. On the left, Dad was holding Tonya's other hand and he looked upset. Not that Teal could blame him. She herself had never seen Tonya like that. It tugged at her heart. It was amazing how, over time, things could change so completely. A couple of years earlier, when she'd met this same woman, she'd wanted nothing to do with her. Teal had feared this woman would try and take her father away from her.

Teal hugged her father first.

As soon as Toby spotted her, he hopped off the bed and came running around the end of the bed toward her. "Teeeeeeeeeeeeeeeeeeeeeee!" he squealed.

Teal loved how he got all excited to see her, and the way he said her name gave her goosebumps. Not that she would ever tell her father or Tonya that.

She picked Toby up, swung him around, set him back down and gave him a high-five.

As Toby crawled back up onto his mother's hospital bed, Teal approached Tonya and placed her hand on her shoulder. Teal didn't want to risk a hug because she wasn't sure if Tonya was in pain or not. This kind of scenario was all new to Teal.

"How are you doing? Are you in any pain?"

Tonya sat up straighter and clasped her hands protectively over her abdomen.

"They gave me something for the pain. I'm comfortable. We're just worried about the baby. I'm only thirty-two weeks along. I still have another eight weeks to go before Peanut is due to arrive." Tonya teared up and reached for a tissue.

Despite the seriousness of the situation, Teal half smiled at Tonya's use of the name "Peanut." Once, Teal had accidentally called her sibling-to-be that, and it had stuck. That's what everyone was currently calling the baby.

Two doctors walked in.

"We need a moment to speak with the two of you," the taller one said.

Teal glanced at her father and nodded. Then she turned to her step-brother. "Toby? Do you want to go with me to get a treat?"

"Yes, Teeee." Toby nearly fell off the hospital bed as he tried to jump into her arms. The offer of a treat, with all its mystery, worked like a charm every time.

"Thanks, Teal." Her father patted her shoulder.

***

Toby sat beside her on the cafeteria bench. Smarties were strewn all over the table and the box was empty. He had one in his mouth as he played with the others. He was nice and quiet right now, and she let him be so she could enjoy it while it lasted.

She was very worried about Tonya and the baby. Peanut needed more time in order to be healthy. What were the chances of the baby being okay if it was born in the next few days?

It was somewhat ironic when Teal thought about it. Here was Tonya, super happy about being a mother again but having complications. Then there was Olive, having been dealt an unplanned pregnancy with an abusive boyfriend.

Teal pulled herself out of her concerned thoughts. She needed to focus on Toby now. Toby, her sweet step-brother, who had been sorting his Smarties into different piles with each color in its own pile. She was impressed so decided to take a picture and send it to her father.

***

Somehow, Teal managed to keep Toby busy for over an hour before heading back to the room. She hoped the doctors were gone, and her parents had more information as to what the next steps would be for Peanut. Teal caught herself referring to her father and Tonya as her parents. It felt good.

No matter what, her father always tried to put on a smile, so his smile on their return didn't necessarily mean they'd received good news.

"There's my smart man." Her father gave Toby a high-five.

Teal was pleased. Obviously, her father had received the photo of Toby and the Smarties. After the high-five, Toby climbed onto the bed beside his mother.

Tonya put her arm around Toby before clearing her throat.

"The plan, as of now, is to keep me here for a week to help keep the baby inside for as long as possible. If things are okay after that, and there are no more symptoms of the baby coming early, I will be able to go home. But I will have to be on bed rest." Tonya shrugged her shoulders.

Teal had a good idea but wasn't entirely sure, so she asked. "What does bed rest mean?"

Her father was the one who replied. "It means exactly that. Tonya will have to stay in bed and rest. She won't be able to take Toby out to the park, run errands or anything like that. If she does, it might trigger an early labor, which we don't want. The longer she can keep the baby inside, the better. Best until she's at least thirty-eight weeks."

"Yikes. That's going to be hard. Are you going to be able to take some time off work, Dad?"

"I can take some time but not too much because I want to be able to be with Tonya and the baby after it's born." Teal's father scratched his head then continued to check stuff on his phone.

Teal knew she'd be expected to help but that was okay. It would be good, though, if she had control of just how much help they'd expect of her and when.

"Dad?"

Her father looked up from his cell phone.

"I can watch Toby for a couple of hours once or twice during the week so you can go run errands, or whatever needs to be done. I'll come over on Sundays, too. Maybe spend the day helping out?"

Tonya cut in. "It would be great if you could throw in a load or two of laundry a week. I don't trust your father." She smiled over at him. "Remember that time you bleached all my new clothes? Who adds bleach to black clothes?"

"Sure," said Teal. "I can do cleaning, throw in a laundry, do dishes, play with Toby." She smiled at her little brother. "Especially play with Toby. And I can take him out so he isn't climbing the walls too much."

"Thanks, honey. It means a lot to me that we can count on you." Her father's hug felt good.

The extra time spent helping out with Toby would

take time away from schoolwork, and Jackson, but it would work out. Besides, maybe Jackson would go with her to her father's a couple of times and take Toby out with her.

41

As soon as Olive walked into the living room, she knew something had happened. The air felt as though her mother had been lurking in ambush. Olive knew from experience this was definitely not a good sign so she sat down on the edge of the couch.

Her mother asked right up front. "When was the exact last time you had any contact with Brad?"

If Brad were the topic, there might be a chance that Olive, herself, wasn't in trouble. Behind her back, she crossed the fingers of both hands, hoping this would be the case.

"The last time I saw him was the day he hit me." Olive made sure her eyes met her mother's so her mother would know she was telling the truth.

"What about the last time you spoke on the phone? Or through text? Or whatever, since that day?" Her mother had both hands on her hips now, and towered over her. Absolutely definitely not a good sign. This always meant things would be taking a turn for the even worse. Olive still wasn't sure exactly why her mother was upset.

"Three days after I spent the night at Teal's, he sent me a text saying he loved me, he was sorry and that it wouldn't happen again. He wanted to know if I could forgive him. And he asked me to visit him in jail up at Innes. Said he had put my name on the visitors' list and everything already."

Olive looked down at the floor. She hadn't lied, but had no idea what was going on so was even less confident about making direct eye contact with her mother.

"And how did you reply?" her mother breathed out slowly.

"I sent one text message back saying it was over and not to contact me again. That was it. Just the one message."

"Nothing else to add?"

"Just what I said. You don't believe me, do you?"

Olive took her cell phone out of her purse and held it up at arm's length so her mother could see it.

"Check if you want. They're there. All the messages from him. You can see for yourself I haven't answered a single one!"

Her mother made no move to take the phone so Olive tossed it onto the couch beside her.

"Zero phone calls, visits or texts since the night he hit you? That's the truth?"

Olive closed her eyes. She wanted to say something about the fact that her mother never seemed to believe her, but thought it best she tread carefully.

"Yes. I swear." Olive unclenched her hands.

"Well, guess what Brad did today?"

Olive sat up straight.

What could he do from jail? Or maybe they'd let him out and he'd come to the house?

"What are you talking about, Mom? What did he do? I swear I had nothing to do with it."

She didn't know how else to convince her mother. She was telling the truth.

"I definitely think you are wrong this time, Olive."

Olive raised her eyebrows. What story was Brad trying to make up now? She didn't know what to say.

"He used the payphone at Innes. Inmates are allowed to do that, you know, and he called here. He asked to speak to you and, of course, I said no. He wanted to talk to you because he told me that he had been doing some thinking and has come up with a few potential names for the baby." Her voice was much louder now.

"Shit," was all Olive managed to say.

She wasn't sure if she should remain seated on the couch or stand up in case she had to run or something. She was both embarrassed and scared at the same time. She stood.

"So it's true. You are pregnant. I don't need to ask how it happened. Tell me you were using something." Her mother quietly sank onto the couch.

Good sign. This meant things were less likely to get heated.

"Of course, Brad and I used something. It just happened. I don't know why but it did. You don't think I'm smart enough to think? I know I'm too young."

Olive sat down again, but as far away from her mother as she could.

"Don't raise your voice at me and don't use his name. You know I can't stand him. I told you before he was up to no good and he will always hold you back. You deserve so much better, Olive."

Olive looked up. It wasn't often her mother paid her a compliment.

"Do you know how far along you are?"

"I think about five or six weeks at the most. I missed my period and a week later, I took the test. I still can't believe it."

"What are you going to do? I can't make the decision for you. It's yours to make. But I *will* try to be supportive."

"I don't know. How much time do I have to figure things out?" Olive asked.

This was overwhelming. Her mother had been eighteen when she'd had Olive.

Her mother shrugged. "I'm not a hundred percent sure but at the most maybe six weeks," she offered.

"That's good. I mean, that's good that I have some time to think about it. I really have no idea what I'm going to do. None of the options seems good."

Olive sank deeper into the couch. She wished she could disappear into it.

Her mother patted Olive's knee. "I just don't want to lose you. You're all that I have in this world. You have your whole life ahead of you."

Somehow, this made Olive feel somewhat better.

42

Teal checked the phone. It was Olive.

"Hey, what's up?"

"My mom knows I am pregnant!"

"You told her? Wow."

"No. I would never have told her. It was Brad. He called here because he wanted to speak to me so we could talk about possible names for our baby."

"You are joking."

"I wish I was, but I am not. I wasn't home so obviously he left that message with my mother. I can't believe he's such a prick."

"Okay, so now what? Are you allowed to leave the house? Is she burning your stuff? Is she going down to the jail to talk some business with Brad? What's going on?" Teal fired question after question at her.

"No. Mom's handling it okay. I still don't know what I'm doing. Mom hasn't mentioned that I was grounded or anything, but if you don't hear from me for a bit, then you'll know she changed her mind."

"Well, at least you don't have to keep it a secret from her anymore." Teal offered. She honestly wasn't sure what else there was to say. "What are you going to do next?" Olive's situation was time sensitive.

"Make an appointment with my doctor and go from there. Maybe she can give me more information on the different options. I know there's stuff out all over the Internet, but this is not something to mess around with."

Teal giggled.

"What's so funny, Teal? Seriously, there's nothing funny going on."

"You, being serious. It's not like you at all. It will take getting used to."

"I don't have a choice, do I? This isn't some small thing. It's huge and can change things for me for the rest of my life. Plus, it's not as if I can just sit and wait for months to figure this one out. It has to be soon."

"I'll come with you to your doctor's appointment if you want me to," Teal offered.

"That would be great. I'll let you know when the appointment is. Thanks."

***

An hour later, Teal received Olive's text with the date and time of the appointment. Olive was giving herself time to think things over. Impressive. Teal wondered if Olive's mother would be invited to come with them.

43

As Teal locked her apartment door, the next-door neighbor opened his. It looked like he was heading out.

Teal nodded in the direction of the elderly man with the cat named Oscar and took the initiative. "Morning, Mister. How are you?"

At first, he didn't say anything, but as she put her keys away in her bag, he answered. "I'm okay thanks."

Before she could say anything else, he was walking fast past her, right out of the apartment building.

Strange, but it was a start. Maybe they would strike up a conversation over the next couple of months.

She headed to her father's place.

Tonya had only three weeks and a couple of days left until the baby was born. This was good. Everything seemed to be going smoothly. If the baby could wait a little longer, they would be out of the woods.

Teal dumped all the clean clothes out of the laundry

basket and onto the bed to fold them. She was nearly half done when Toby ran into the room.

"Tee. Candy!" Toby said, giving her his best but-I'm-so-cute smile.

It was Teal's own fault. A couple weeks ago, she had bought a box of Fruit by the Foot and Toby had fallen in love with them. The candy was like Play-Doh. It could be molded, and you could eat it as well.

They were waiting for Olive and then the three of them were going to the park for a while to give Tonya a break.

Teal's father was at work and wouldn't be back any time soon.

An elderly woman, Stella, on the ground floor of one of the buildings he supervised, had forgotten she was cooking something on the stove when she went to her friend Pippy's three doors down and asked to visit and have tea.

Stella and Pippy had just sat down to enjoy their tea when the building's fire alarm went off. It wasn't until after the fire department had arrived and gone into the apartment to put out the fire that she realized it was all happening in her apartment.

It was Teal's father's job to figure out everything that needed to be done.

Teal would have her cell phone on in case Tonya needed anything, and the park was only a fifteen-minute walk from the apartment.

A knock sounded at the door. When Teal looked through the peephole, Olive stuck out her tongue.

Laughing, Teal opened the door and as soon as Toby

saw Olive, he chanted, "Live, Live, Live."

"Give me a high-five, Toby!"

Toby slapped twice, once on each hand.

"Let's head out," Teal said, then called to Tonya. "We're leaving now."

"Okay. Thanks." Tonya yelled back.

***

At the park, Toby sat on the swing for a bit then decided he wanted to play in the sand and make things with his blue shovel and bucket and his molds.

Olive and Teal sat with him and mindlessly dug or drew X's and O's in the sand.

"How are you really doing?" Teal asked, as she looked Olive directly in the eye.

"Could be better. Plus, the run-in with Brad's mother, Marlene, kind of shook Mom up."

"What? I didn't know about that." Teal was genuinely surprised this had somehow gotten past her.

"Seriously,? You didn't know?"

"Mom never said anything."

Teal found it hard to believe that her mother had purposely held something back. Her mother loved to take ordinary situations and use them as a life lessons for Teal. Her mother never missed an opportunity.

"Yikes. Guess my mom is keeping it on the down low big time if she didn't mention it to yours. A good thing, I guess. The less people know, the better. I have enough to deal with. I don't need any fuel added to the fire. As they say."

"Come on. So what happened?"

Clap. Clap. Clap. Toby was proud. "It's a cassile!" he exclaimed.

"It's absolutely beautiful," Teal told him quickly and patted his head before turning back to Olive.

The conversation continued.

"Mom was doing groceries, minding her own business, then all of a sudden, she feels a tap on her left shoulder. She turns around and it's Marlene. Mom knows who Marlene is, of course, so she says 'Hi.'

"Then Marlene puts her hands on her hips and starts telling Mom that I told lies about my pregnancy. How, that even if I *was* pregnant, we'd never know who the baby daddy was because of all the men I've dated. That Mom needs to keep me away from her Brad."

Teal put her hand over her mouth to try to suppress her giggle, but it didn't work very well. "So did your mom smack her across the face?"

This brought a smile to Olive's worried face.

Beside them, Toby began to flatten his castles with a few of the cars he'd brought along with him.

"She told me she felt like it but managed to control herself." A full smile from Olive now. "She told Marlene to mind her own damn business and if she ever spoke to her like that again she would personally guarantee there would *not* be another run-in. Ever."

"That's crazy. Hopefully that family leaves you alone."

After a couple more sandcastles, Toby lost interest and wanted to go on the swing. Teal and Olive pushed him back and forth and continued to chat.

"How are things between you and Jackson?"

Teal couldn't help but blush. She still couldn't believe someone would be interested in her. Yet they were still together. "Still going well. We're good." She almost went on about what a great guy he was but that would have made Olive flinch for sure. "So you're hanging in there? How *are* things between you and your mom? Tell me the truth."

For a moment, Olive didn't say anything. She pushed Toby a couple more times, then answered. "It's complicated. My emotions are all over the place. Sometimes Mom seems supportive and other times, when she looks at me, I can see disappointment all over her face, and it hurts. It really hurts. More than Brad ever hurt me. I don't know if that makes any sense to you at all. It's hard." Olive looked like she was about to cry.

"It's hard for your mom, as well."

Teal tried to give Olive a winning smile but she must not have been convincing because Olive didn't acknowledge it.

"Things'll get back on track. It takes time."

"Actually, I feel a little off right now. Can we go back to Toby's place?"

"Sure. It's been nearly two hours. We must have worn Toby out at least a little bit. When we get in, we can always pop in one of his fave movies, make popcorn and guaranteed, he'll be asleep fifteen minutes into the movie."

Teal loaded all the sandbox toys into the bag.

44

BACK AT HER FATHER'S APARTMENT, Teal and Olive heard a weird noise. Teal looked at Olive quickly and ran to Tonya's bedroom.

Tonya had curled herself up, almost into a ball. She let out a moan.

Olive rushed to her side.

Tonya's eyes met with hers. She smiled weakly.

"What's going on? Are you okay?" Teal asked, panicked.

"I'm pretty sure it's time. My water broke." Tonya looked around at the wet mess all over the bed.

"You serious. Why didn't you call me?" Teal tried to help Tonya move out of the wet zone of the mattress to a drier area.

"I was going to but as I reached for my cell phone, I accidentally knocked it off my bed." Tonya pointed to the floor on the right side of the bed.

Teal reached down and picked up the phone. She used Tonya's thumb to unlock it, scrolled the contacts and found her father's number, then called.

As his phone started ringing, she put the phone on speaker so she could multi-task. The last thing she needed was the baby to pop out right there. That was not happening!

Luckily, on top of Tonya's diaper bag, still packed since she'd been at the hospital before, was an outfit for Tonya to wear. Teal quickly grabbed it and handed it to Tonya who stood up and started pacing, her face wincing.

Teal's father still hadn't answered his phone. No doubt things were even worse at the fire site than he'd originally thought.

After that contraction passed, Tonya sat on the bed again to take her clothes off and put on the dry ones. Teal turned away and fiddled with the diaper bag, adjusting things. She didn't want to embarrass Tonya by watching her dress, but she didn't feel right leaving her in the bedroom alone in case she fell or something.

A couple minutes later Tonya was dressed, Teal had the diaper bag, and they were in the living room.

Olive looked nervous. "Is your dad on his way?"

"He's not answering. And I don't think it's a good idea to wait. I think we should go to the hospital."

"Okay… And just how are you getting there? What about Toby?"

"Oh," said Teal. It was a good question.

"Okay. I know. Teal? You go to the hospital with Tonya and I'll stay here and watch Toby. If you want, I can keep trying to reach your dad."

"Awesome. That would be great. That will save us the worry about Toby. Now I just need to figure out how to get her to the hospital."

Teal glanced over at Tonya who had the car keys in her hand and was heading for the door.

"I've only driven a couple of times," Teal said, "but I do have my G1. The hospital's not super far. I could give it a shot."

"Not happening." Tonya hunched over with another contraction. "Thanks, Olive. You're a dear. We'll be fine. Please don't worry. I'll call later with an update."

Tonya hugged Toby who then took her hand as though he expected to be going with her. Tonya leaned down to explain that he had to stay home and wait for his little sister or brother to show up. That she needed to go to the hospital for that to happen. Once Toby heard the word hospital, he settled down and went back to the living room to look for a movie he and Olive could watch.

When Teal hugged Olive goodbye, she whispered a thank you then she and Tonya headed out.

The drive to the hospital was one of the worst rides Teal had ever experienced. Tonya would drive normally for a bit, then a contraction would take hold and it was a struggle. Sometimes she would start speeding up or brake too fast and she even ran a stop sign.

Finally, after nearly forty minutes, they arrived at the hospital, and in one piece. Miraculously, a security guard had been roaming around the parking lot and helped them nab a parking spot within a short time. At the entrance door, Teal grabbed a wheelchair and helped Tonya get into it. She'd left the diaper bag in the trunk along with the suitcase. She figured they were not needed right away.

Tonya instructed her to the maternity ward. The woman at the desk was super nice. Teal appreciated this as she had no idea what she was doing.

After the receptionist informed them that Tonya was in labor—as if that wasn't obvious—Teal thought it best to answer when a question was asked as it didn't seem like Tonya was up to the task.

Finally, once Tonya was helped into a gown and settled in a delivery room, Teal was able to relax.

She tried calling her father again, but still couldn't get through. She sent Olive a text letting her know they had made it to the hospital and thanked her again for watching Toby.

Olive replied with a quick "Welcome."

A nurse came into the room, announced that her name was Gillian, and that she had just started her shift.

Teal stayed by Tonya's side but felt absolutely useless. There wasn't any point in calling her father every thirty seconds, either. She would keep trying but she needed to be there for Tonya. Besides, Olive was continuing to try to get through to him.

Teal's job right now was to make sure Tonya was as comfortable as she could possibly be.

Teal put her hand on the bed near Tonya. "Is there anything I can do to help?"

Tonya grabbed her hand and squeezed it. "Just your being here is a big help."

The nurse smiled at them. "It's nice your daughter's here to witness the birth of her sibling. A rare but exciting opportunity indeed."

Tonya and Teal locked eyes and smiled. Neither bothered to correct the nurse. It didn't matter now. By now, it didn't matter at all.

45

It was just before she received Teal's text letting her know they'd arrived at the hospital, when she felt it: a sharp pain in her lower abdomen.

Olive was on the couch with Toby but there was still room to stretch out. That helped. Maybe it was stress or something, so it was best to relax. The movie *Moana* was playing. This was good. Toby would be distracted—quiet—for the next while. Maybe he would even fall asleep. As long as he was quiet, all would be good. Right now, she had to get herself comfortable.

To take her mind off her discomfort, she would try once again to reach Teal's father. No luck.

Toby was a sweet kid. He really was. Until recently, she had never even thought of having kids or not having kids. It was a topic that hadn't crossed her mind. To be fair, though, she was too young. Seeing Toby and spending time with him, as well as the whole pregnancy thing, had really slammed into her. The thought was there constantly now. Plus, there was a huge urgency for her to make a decision. No matter what she thought about her situation, when it came down to the choices, she didn't like any of them. So how then was she supposed to be confident that she would make the right decision? How was she supposed to live with that decision? She already knew the answer to her own question. No matter the decision, she would have to live with it the rest of her life. And it would haunt her.

***

Teal couldn't help but glance over at the entrance to the delivery room every so often. Where was her father? Of course he had the emergency at work but this was important, too. More so. There must be someone who could take over for a while so he could come to the hospital. Teal had never seen Tonya angry and she wanted to keep it that way if she had anything to do with it.

"Where's your dad?" Tonya asked as another contraction hit.

"He's on his way." Teal lied without hesitation, thinking if she kept Tonya calm, everything would work out fine.

"As soon as this contraction is over," said Gillian, the nurse, who was almost constantly at Tonya's bedside, "I'm going to check again to see how far you're dilated."

Tonya and Teal's eyes locked, then Teal left the room to give Tonya and Gillian privacy for a moment.

She called back. "I'll call him again right now, Tonya. Just try to relax, okay?"

Then at last, her father's voice.

Outside the hospital room, Teal tapped her foot impatiently. "Where are you? Are you on your way?"

"Teal! No, I'm not off work yet. I don't get off until… What's going on? Is everything okay?"

"Dad! Don't you ever check your messages? Didn't Olive talk to you? Get to the hospital. Now!"

As people passed by, they glanced at her with raised eyebrows. Teal didn't care.

"Hospital? Oh my gosh." Her father's voice rose. "It's Tonya? She's having the baby?"

"Yes. Took you long enough to catch on. Her water broke a while ago. They're checking her dilation again. Whatever that means. That's what the nurse said, anyway. You need to be here. That's all I know."

"I am on my way. Tell her not to move. To wait for me."

Teal laughed. Where was Tonya going to go at this stage?

"Sure, Dad. I'll tell her. And bring me a coffee or something. Bring me anything. Maybe you should bring something for yourself, too. This isn't easy. Love ya. Bye."

Teal hung up before her father could ask any more questions. Then she made a quick call to her mother to let her know where she was, and not to expect her home anytime soon. After Tonya had the baby, she would want to stay for a bit.

Next on the list was Olive, but there was no response to Teal's text.

What was Olive's problem, now? She'd been left

with only a couple of responsibilities. All she had to do was: one, watch Toby, who was probably asleep; and two, get hold of Teal's father, which she had obviously not done. It wasn't as if Teal ever asked a whole lot of Olive—ever. Today was different, though. She had counted on Olive. But maybe Olive had fallen asleep on the couch, cuddled with Toby, while watching a movie, as Teal often did herself. That was possible. She would try again later.

***

Back in the hospital room, Teal met with Tonya's questioning face.

"He'd better be on his way."

Teal had to smile. She had never seen this side of Tonya before. She rather liked it. "Yeah. He is. No worries. He'll be here. Just do what they tell you."

While Teal had been out of the room making phone calls, the nurse had checked Tonya. They were nearly there. It was almost time to push. So far, Tonya had refused to take anything for the pain, but the pain seemed to be getting worse, and the baby was still inside. How much longer could Tonya hold out?

"You sure you don't want anything for the pain?" Gillian asked Tonya.

Tonya stared at her.

"I'm only asking because soon it will be time to start pushing. I thought I'd ask now because soon, even if you want pain medication, it will be too late. I have to keep asking."

"I'm fine. It doesn't tickle but I think I'll be okay."

Teal admired her for saying no to pain medication. As she watched Tonya, she'd already decided that when the time came for *her* to have kids, she would *definitely* take pain medication. As far as she knew, no special awards were given out to women who had all-natural births.

"Uh oh," Tonya said, looking at Teal.

"What's wrong?"

Gillian rushed to Tonya's side.

"Tell me. What's going on?" Gillian insisted.

"I feel like I have to push, but he isn't here yet. He's going to miss the whole damn thing!"

When Tonya squeezed her fingers into a fist, Teal wondered if this was because her father wasn't there yet, or if the pain had worsened. Either way, it wasn't a good sign.

Struggling, Tonya moved around on the bed, Teal guessed it was to make herself feel more comfortable.

A commotion in the hall made all three of them turn toward the door. Teal's father flew into the room, almost tripping over his own feet, but miraculously not spilling his tray of three Tim Horton's Iced Capps.

Half an hour later, Teal's baby sister arrived weighing five pounds, eleven ounces. Not bad considering she was a few weeks early. Teal couldn't believe how beautiful she was.

Now that her father was there, it was time to find out what was up with Olive. She couldn't wait to tell her they'd named the baby Violet Teal Flint. The "Teal" part, after her.

46

As gently as she could, Olive slid Toby off her and onto the couch. He stayed asleep. Good. She didn't have to worry about him for the moment. She slipped a blanket over him.

She had thought for sure after she'd taken something for the pain in her abdomen, that it would have gone away, but it was being persistent.

After propping a cushion in front of Toby, she made her way to the bathroom. She sat on the toilet and closed her eyes. It was only when she opened them again that she noticed the blood in her underwear. She shouldn't be having her period. She was pregnant. She had read somewhere that some women spotted throughout their pregnancies, but this was not the case here. This was not spotting.

Olive swept her left foot closer to the bathroom door, the door opened further. She could see Toby from where she was on the toilet. He was still asleep. Definitely good. She could not deal with him. Not right now. Another pain. Olive clutched her abdomen. This couldn't be her period. If it was, this pain was something she wasn't accustomed to. Normally, she was grumpy during her time of the month, but rarely did she ever have to take something for discomfort. She counted to ten, then stood up. She wiped herself and then rummaged around in the bathroom until she found exactly what she needed: a sanitary napkin. She put one on. Tonya probably wouldn't notice, nor would Teal if it was hers.

She made her way back to the couch and slowly cuddled up against Toby. She was glad she wasn't alone. She hoped that Tonya and the baby were doing okay. Hard to believe that Teal was going to be a big sister. Things sure had changed a lot in the last couple of years. Olive and Teal were still friends and that was a good sign. Something she still appreciated: their friendship.

Suddenly, it dawned on Olive. Maybe she was having a miscarriage!

She quickly picked up her phone and Googled articles such as *signs you are having a miscarriage*. According to her calculation, she was between eight and ten weeks pregnant.

Toby stirred in his sleep but his eyes remained shut. Good.

She continued to scroll through articles. Within half an hour, she had her answer. There would be no hard choice to make. Olive would not have to decide if she wanted to keep the baby and raise it on her own, have the baby and give it up for adoption, or have an abortion.

The choice—if you could even call it that—had been made for her. She had lost the baby. A tear from each cheek fell. It didn't matter that she hadn't known what she'd wanted. What mattered was the choice had been snatched away from her. She was no longer pregnant.

How ironic that her best friend was at the hospital waiting to greet her new sibling and here she was, having just lost her child. Olive quietly sobbed.

***

Olive must have drifted off to sleep. Next thing she knew, she felt something furry brush against her leg. She slowly opened one eye, then the other.

Toby had a paintbrush in one hand and a jar of something else in the other.

Just as he dipped the brush into the jar, Olive bolted straight up. What was he up to? Cripes. Had she actually fallen asleep while she babysat Toby? Not good at all.

She listened for a moment, but didn't hear anything. The good news was, it was still just the two of them in the apartment. She fought back tears as she realized she needed to change her pad again.

"Hey, Toby. Wha'cha got there?" The last thing she wanted to do was upset him.

"Paint!" He clapped his hands. This caused whatever was in the jar to slosh around and spill over the side of the jar.

Olive braced herself for blood red paint to appear.

Clear. The liquid coming out of the jar was clear. Lucky for her, Toby hadn't actually gotten into the paint yet.

"You want to paint, buddy?" Olive slowly rose from the couch. She felt somewhat better than she had earlier.

"Yep. Paint please. I got the stuff. I just need colors now!" Toby walked toward the dining room table.

"Give me a minute and I'll set everything up. I just have to go to the bathroom first."

"Okay. Potty first." Toby nodded his head in her direction.

In the bathroom she changed the pad again. Maybe the whole thing was over. Not that it was something she would be able to forget anytime soon, but seeing the blood linger would just be a constant reminder. That was the last thing she needed.

47

Teal couldn't believe her baby sister, Violet, had finally arrived. When her father had asked if she wanted to hold the baby, of course, she'd said "Yes!" But she couldn't believe how small the baby was compared to Toby. She was used to his weight in her arms, not a newborn baby's.

After only a moment, it was clear that her father wanted the baby back.

Although she was reluctant to hand the baby over, she did. It was time, anyway, for her to first call her mother to let her know the baby had arrived safely, and then to check in with Olive to see how she was faring with Toby.

***

"How are things going with Toby?"

"Things are good. We just started painting."

Normally Olive would have kept chatting. What was going on with her? Teal thought it a bit strange. "Is everything okay, Olive? Is Toby giving you a hard time?" Teal couldn't think what else could be going on. Or maybe it had something had to do with Brad. Oh gosh. Not Brad. Teal couldn't deal with that crap now. All she wanted to do was bask in the sunlight of her new baby sister. Couldn't she just enjoy these moments?

"Nope."

A one-word answer. Olive had confirmed it. Teal knew for sure now that something was up. Part of her wanted to leave it alone but part of her knew it would keep bothering her until she found out was going on. Also, what if something major needed to be dealt with right now and couldn't wait?

Teal decided not to take the chance.

"Olive. We've been friends for a long time. I don't believe you."

Nothing but silence on the other end for a full five seconds. In fact, Teal thought maybe they had been disconnected. She checked her phone but it looked like the they were both still on the line.

"Olive? You there?"

"Yeah. Don't worry about things over here. Toby's fine. Is it there yet?"

"What?" Just like Olive to change topics. Good tactic.

"The baby!"

"Yes. And she's so cute. They named her Violet Teal Flint. Isn't that so cool? My name is her middle name."

"Baby! Baby! Baby!"

Teal laughed as she heard Toby squeal in the background. He must have heard Olive as they talked about the baby.

Teal heard Olive talking to Toby: "Yes, your baby sister is coming home soon."

She heard Toby clap his hands twice.

"Yippee! Tee?"

"Looks like he wants to chat with you, Teal. Is that okay?"

"Definitely. Put him on the phone."

Of course Teal didn't mind spending a moment or two on the phone with Toby. That way, she'd even have more to report to her father. That worked out. Two birds with one stone kind of deal.

"Baby sister?" Toby asked.

"Yep. She's here and will be coming home soon. Now you make sure you're a good boy for Olive. Okay? Your baby sister will need a good brother. Can you do that, Toby?"

"Yes!" Toby exclaimed and clapped his hands again.

"Let me talk to Olive again. Ex Oh."

"Ess Oh."

Then Olive's voice. "It's me."

"Sounds like things are going good with Toby. But Olive, I wish you'd tell me what's going on with you. If it's Brad, just tell me."

"Why do you automatically think it has to do with Brad? I told you it's over between us. You honestly think I would go back to him after what he did to me? I cannot believe you would think that." Teal could hear Olive's deeply inhaled breath.

Teal tried smoothing things over. "Come on, Olive. I'm sorry but it's not like you haven't gone back to him before. I just want to make sure you're safe and okay. To me, if you're back with him, then you're not safe and you're far from okay. Okay?"

She sensed that Olive wasn't really angry. It sounded like her friend was ready to break into sobs. They both had a lot on their plates right now.

"Just enjoy your time at the hospital with Violet and tell your dad and Tonya I said congrats. I will hold the fort down as long as they need me to."

"Thanks a bunch. I'll be home shortly to help out."

Teal hung up.

She had hoped to keep Olive on the phone longer, thinking her friend would eventually give in and tell her what was wrong, but the plan hadn't worked. Olive hadn't given her the slightest clue what might be going on. At least things seemed to be okay with Toby, and he wasn't giving Olive too much of a hard time. This was good. One less thing to worry about.

A few hours later, Teal's father indicated he wanted to spend the night at the hospital with the baby and Tonya.

The hospital staff strongly discouraged him, and Tonya finally convinced him to go home since Toby was there, and it would be best if at least one of them was around for him.

Obviously, for the moment, it couldn't be Tonya and it wasn't fair to expect both Olive and Teal to drop everything to look after Toby for them indefinitely even though Olive had said everything was going okay and that she didn't really mind staying. The fact was, Teal had already told her mother that she wouldn't be home tonight. She planned to spend the night at her father's to keep him company and to help with Toby.

48

TEAL HADN'T EVEN HAD TIME to take off her shoes before Toby barreled out of the kitchen. At least he'd remembered to leave his paint brush behind before running up to her.

"Baby sister. Baby sister." Toby looked around as he tugged on Teal's pants.

Teal's father scooped Toby into his arms but Toby stared down the hallway toward the entrance door, seemingly determined to figure out where his baby sister was.

"You kids eat?" asked her father.

Olive shook her head. "I wasn't sure what time you'd be home."

Teal watched Olive. She hadn't been able to shake the feeling that something had happened while they were at the hospital.

Toby chipped in once again. "Baby sister. Baby sister. Where baby sister?"

"He definitely seems ready to meet his baby sister," Teal said, laughing.

"Let's order in supper," Teal's father waved his iPad. "Pizza good for everyone?"

Teal decided to let her father explain to Toby where his baby sister was. It would be easier that way.

"Your baby sister—her name is Violet—is with Mommy. They are sleeping at the hospital tonight, but will be home soon."

"Why is Mommy at hospital? Does she have a bobo?" Toby's eyes widened.

"A small one. She has a bobo because she had your baby sister. You remember her name is Violet?" Dad explained. Poorly.

"She is bad baby sister?" Toby's chin quivered. He was near tears. "Gave Mommy bobo?"

"No, Toby. She's not a bad baby sister." Teal said as she cleared the paint mess off the kitchen table to prepare a space for everyone to eat when the pizza arrived.

Teal's father turned to face Olive. "You will stay for supper, won't you, Olive? I know it's late, but…"

"I can't. But thanks for the offer. Lots of schoolwork to do. There's just never enough hours in the day." Olive picked up her shoes, put them on and started lacing them up.

Teal knew that Olive was lying through her teeth. Her father hadn't spent as much time with Olive as Teal's mother had. She knew her mother would have caught the lie in a heartbeat. Never had Olive ever used "too much schoolwork" as an excuse for anything in her entire life. School wasn't a priority for Olive. She did what she needed to get by and that was about it.

Just as Olive was about to leave, Teal hugged her and Teal was surprised that Olive held onto her longer than usual.

"Message me later and thanks a bunch for helping out with Toby," Teal told her.

"No worries. Can't wait to meet the new addition to the family. And yes, I'll message you later."

***

Throughout supper, Teal had waited for a message to come through from Olive. It hadn't. And now it was almost midnight and still nothing from Olive.

Teal couldn't wait any longer. She had to send her a message because, if not, Olive would probably assume that Teal wasn't worried, and that simply wasn't true. Teal had been busy at the hospital with her sister, true, but she'd still known something was going on. Something that wasn't good. Something had upset Olive and it looked like whatever had happened, had nothing to do with Brad. Teal was definitely stumped.

> I'll give you space if that's what you want. But I know something's wrong.-T

Half an hour later Olive finally messaged her.

> Thanks. Sorry.-O

It was unusual for Olive to apologize. Something that wasn't generally in her nature.

> Olive, I am worried about you.-T

> I lost it.-O

Well, Olive had every reason to have lost it, Teal thought. She had so much on her plate already. Add the fact that Brad, being an ass, had called from jail to talk to Olive's mom and had ratted Olive out. Not good. Not good at all. Teal empathized with her friend. Normally, Teal would trade places with her friend Olive in a heartbeat. Not this time. Currently her own life looked good compared to Olive's.

> Don't be upset. It can't be helped.-T

> How could you be so insensitive?-O

> I don't mean to be. I'm just saying you have every right to be upset. You have a lot going on.

> What Brad did by calling your mom and telling her, was unforgivable. And horrible. I can't even imagine what you are going through.-T

Half an hour went by.

Teal typed out another message.

> What's going on, Olive? I just wanted to make sure you were okay. Please tell me what I can do to help.-T

> I'm sorry. I misunderstood what you said. I thought you were happy about what happened with the baby.-O

> The baby? Wha—?Oh my gosh. What happened? Are you okay? What's going on? Want me to come over?-T

> No! I don't want to be around anyone right now. I just need to be left alone. The baby is gone.-O

> Olive. Listen to me. The last thing I want to do is

> upset you but I don't understand what you're talking about. What happened?-T

> I miscarried while you were at the hospital with Tonya. Please. Please. I don't want to talk about it. No matter what. Please don't make me.-O

Teal dropped her phone onto the bed. Oh my gosh. As if. While she had been off helping—or at least being there for Tonya at the hospital—Olive had been here. Alone with Toby. And she had miscarried. How horrible it must have been. It had probably been for the best but that wasn't the point. The point was the pain Olive had endured on her own. In addition, how the choice of what to do had been stolen from her.

> Olive, I am so sorry. No matter what, I am so sorry. Let me know if there's anything I can do.-T

Teal waited an hour then gave up. No reply. Had Olive told her mother yet? Teal figured it was best for now if she left Olive alone. She would check in on her in the morning. That was all she could do.

49

AFTER TEAL HAD DEBATED most of the night, all the while tossing and turning, she decided it was best to show up at Olive's house unannounced. She was afraid that if Olive were forewarned, she wouldn't answer the door or, more likely, she'd make sure she wasn't at home in the first place. The element of surprise was best in any situation involving Olive.

Olive's mother opened the door after the first knock. Teal looked her up and down. She couldn't tell if she knew what had happened or not. Best to act like everything was cool. Cool. Yeah. She could play cool. No worries.

As Teal entered Olive's bedroom, Teal's cell phone went off. She quickly checked. It was a message from Jackson.

> I was thinking, maybe I could go with you?-J

Where? To the prom?-T

Uh. No. To Spain! Spend time with you before classes start.-J

Teal didn't know what to reply. She wanted to take this trip on her own. Not with Jackson. Yikes. This was not something she had expected. Not at all. Why hadn't he brought up that idea months ago? Not now, with her leaving in a few weeks. Talk about waiting until the last minute.

She inhaled deeply. For now, it didn't matter. She was here at Olive's. For Olive. The rest she would have to figure out later.

Olive was sitting on her bed, wrapped in an old comforter that Teal recognized from their younger days. Olive would always bring that very same pink-and-white-striped comforter with her on sleepovers.

Teal pointed at it. "Blast from the past, eh?"

"Hmm."

This was not a very good start. Teal sat on the edge of the bed.

Two full minutes went by during which neither of them said anything.

Finally, since she couldn't figure out what else to do, Teal moved in closer and pulled Olive into a hug. It wasn't long before Olive's shoulders started shaking and the tears came.

"It's going to be okay," Teal said. "I know it sucks right now, but it's going to be okay. It'll just take time. Maybe a lot of time. Well, maybe lots of time, but you know what I mean." Teal shush-shushed her.

Olive sobbed so hard, she was gasping.

"I don't know how you feel and I'm not going to pretend I do. But I do know that the last few months have been crappy for you. Really crappy. This happened, and the stuff with Brad just added to it."

Teal pushed Olive back so she could glance around for a box of tissues. She spotted them on the dresser and released Olive to reach out for them.

Olive grabbed a handful and blew her nose several times.

Better on the tissues than on me. Teal continued. "We have the prom next week. Hooray! Right?" She didn't feel all that enthusiastic herself about it right now, but needed to do something to get Olive to react. She didn't want to see Olive skip the prom and regret it later on, on top of everything else.

"Big whoop." Olive's eyes locked with hers.

"Come on. You have your dress and everything," Teal reminded her.

"Yeah, but I'm kinda short a date, remember? Brad's not supposed to be around me."

"Well, yes. There is that restraining order but that's beside the point. You need to let him go." Teal stood up and folded her arms across her chest.

"Easy for you to say. You have Jackson."

"Yep, and this is the first guy I have ever really dated. I waited a long time. Olive, you've dated a few and Brad is not the one for you. I may not have as much experience as you when it comes to relationships, but I know if a guy actually cares for you, he doesn't ever hit you. No matter *what*."

"I guess."

"You guess? You guess? What are you talking about? You think I'm making this up? That I'm lying?" Teal was getting more and more frustrated with her friend. Would she ever understand how bad Brad was for her?

"I just meant that you have Jackson. Who's amazing, by the way. And you're going on that trip. And you have a new sister. Lots of good things are going on for you. And my life is shit right now."

"I agree with you, Olive. Your life *is* shit right now. But why is it that way? Did you ever ask yourself that? Why?" By now, Teal was swaying back and forth from foot to foot. Things were getting heated.

Suddenly, Olive threw back the comforter and slid off the bed. She rose to her full height, angry eyes locked with Teal's. "Are you saying this is *my* fault? What kind of friend are you?"

Maybe it was time for Teal to speak up. Maybe it was time to tell her friend, Olive, she needed to take responsibility for her own actions.

"The stuff with Brad, yes. He has treated you like crap from the beginning and you just kept going back. *That* is on you. He cheated on you and you took him back. *That* is on you, too. How did he treat you when he found out you were pregnant? What kind of guy does that?"

"I don't want to talk about it." Olive sat back down on the bed.

"Fine. We won't. I'm sorry about the baby, though. I truly am. But you deserve so much better than Brad, Olive. You're my friend. I want you to be happy and safe. You can't have those things with Brad or anyone else who treats you the way he did. You just can't."

"It's not fair!" Olive picked up her purse and threw it against the wall.

Thud.

Within seconds, Olive's mother was in the room. "What's going on here? What are you two fighting about?"

"Nothing." Olive replied.

Teal stared at Olive. It wasn't Teal's place to say anything. This wasn't her mother and she wasn't Olive.

Olive's mother looked from Teal to Olive and back.

Olive didn't say a word.

"I see. That's how it's going to be then. No one wants to talk. Hmm Well, then. I think I shall sit here until someone does. Something is very wrong right here in Derry." She lowered herself to the computer chair and crossed her legs.

Teal couldn't help but smile. She hadn't heard Olive's mom use that quote in a long time. It was from one of Stephen King's movies. She and Olive had watched the movie *It* together several years ago. One weekend during the summer, they had watched a dozen Stephen King movies and had picked up a few quotes they liked. She couldn't remember many of them now, but she remembered that one.

Olive was looking down so it was hard to read the expression on her face.

Teal figured, if Olive's mom knew about the miscarriage, she would have already said something by now. So maybe she didn't know. However, it wasn't Teal's place to tell her, was it? It had to come from her own daughter.

No one said anything, so being there was becoming awkward.

Teal decided it was best if she broke the ice. She had nothing to lose.

"Olive, does your mom know?"

Olive's mother quickly glanced in Teal's direction.

Olive shook her head.

"Do I know what? Would someone tell me what is going on please?"

Olive's mother uncrossed her legs and now sat straight in the chair. Perhaps she sensed this was a more-serious matter, not just two friends arguing over a hot guy.

Olive's mom stared at her but Teal wasn't going to give it up. Olive was the one who had to tell her.

Olive shook her head again. Then, lifting her head and looking at her mother with tear-filled eyes, she spoke up. "The baby. Gone. Happy now?"

"What are you talking about?"

"I lost the baby. Gone. Poof. Hope you're happy now."

Olive's mother got up from the chair and went to the bed where Olive was slouched, before her eyes asked Teal a question.

Teal nodded yes, as in yes, it was true.

It was time for Teal to make her exit.

50

THE ISSUE WITH OLIVE had been taken care of, so now Teal had to figure out what to say to Jackson.

> Very sweet of you! I will be okay on my own.-T
>
> Oh. You don't want me to come with you?-J
>
> It's not that. It's my first trip and I planned to go alone.-T

The last thing Teal wanted to do was have him be mad at her, especially with the prom exactly one week away. But at the same time, she planned on going to Spain alone. Her mother had gone with her to buy her plane tickets last month. Teal had made plans with Dottie. Everything was all set. She was good to go. By herself.

> Okay. Fine then.-J

Teal was still new at relationships, but she knew that

when she herself said something of that nature, it meant everything was far from "fine." Okay. So Jackson was upset. She couldn't do anything about it.

> Will chat with you tonight. xo-T

Teal hoped he would be in a better mood when they chatted later. They usually spoke on the phone for several minutes before they went to bed.

Good. The limo company had confirmed the pick-up time for Jackson and her for prom night. Teal had already picked up her dress, a beautiful wine-red color. The dress hung waiting for her in its own sleek slipcover. Teal had never owned anything so elegant. Jackson had rented a red Calvin Klein tuxedo to match. He wouldn't be able to pick up his tuxedo until the day before prom. Which was fine.

Shortly after supper Olive sent Teal a text message.

> Thanks for today.-O
>
> How are things? How are you doing?-T
>
> Mom and I talked. Still hurts but better. If that makes any sense? lol-O
>
> Yep! It does. I'm glad. Let me know if you need anything.-T
>
> I won't be at school for the activities and stuff.-O
>
> Are you going to be okay at home alone?-T
>
> No worries. Mom is going to spend the day with me..-O
>
> Awesome. Much needed, I think. Any plans?-T
>
> Going to get my hair and nails done.-O

> Take care of yourself.-T
>
> I will. xo-O
>
> xo-T

It would be a good starting-over point for Olive. Teal crossed her fingers that the togetherness of mom and daughter for the day would do them good. She couldn't remember the last time Olive had mentioned that she'd spent time with her mother.

After supper, she'd expected a text from Jackson as was usual, just to see what she was doing, but she didn't get one. Only because he was probably busy, she told herself and tried not to think about it.

Instead, she focused on the prom and her upcoming trip. After prom, she would officially start counting down the days until she left. All she could think of was one word to describe how she felt: free. She couldn't wait to experience what that would actually feel like. Free from school, free from her parents, free from Jackson, free from everything.

After watching an episode of *The Walking Dead*, Teal decided to hop in the shower and then, if she hadn't received a text from Jackson, she would just call. Easier that way.

So of course, she showered more quickly than usual and stubbed her toe as she tried to hurry out of the bathroom to get to her room and check her phone, but no message. No matter, she told herself as she hurriedly dried herself and grabbed a pair of pajamas out of the drawer and slipped them on.

No answer. She ended up calling Jackson three times

and all three times the call had gone straight to voicemail.

She tried to convince herself he was busy but deep down, she wondered if maybe he didn't want to talk to her. Maybe he really was mad because she wanted to go on this trip alone. That was silly. Wasn't it? But what if he was? And what if they ended up breaking up? Or not going to the prom together? What would she do then? She let out a small sob. As if this would really happen. Maybe things were too good to be true.

Next morning, the first thing Teal did was check her phone to see if there was a message from Jackson.

Nothing.

She didn't want to move or get out of bed, but she had to. Today, she was going to her father's to spend the night. Probably one of the second or last times she would see everyone at her father's place before she left for her trip. Months ago, her trip seemed like it was years away. Hard to believe, that this time next month, she would be in another country, exploring on her own. She couldn't wait. School was pretty much over. The prom was in a couple of days. Everything was nearly perfect. Except with whatever was going on between Jackson and her. Whatever that was. She was going to be away for an entire month. Maybe she would leave and he would break up with her through text. All these what ifs were driving her nuts. She got out of bed to get ready to go visit her father.

51

Toby seemed to be extra happy to see her. No doubt because her father and Tonya were busy with Violet and didn't have as much time for one-on-one with him. After she read him a third book, Teal suggested he get out his coloring stuff to make a picture for his baby sister.

Toby jumped at the idea.

That was good. Seeing Toby was great, but she also wanted to spend time with Violet as well.

Violet's little fingers were curled around Teal's left index finger even though the baby was sound asleep. Toby was working hard on a second picture for his sister. And Teal's father and Tonya had gone for a quick coffee for a respite. So far so good.

***

It had been an hour and nothing major had happened. Teal had everything under control and sighed contentedly. She would miss these two while she was gone. Not too much would change with Toby, but the baby would grow while she was in Spain.

Then. A text message! From Jackson!

She stared at the phone wanting to read the message but worried about what it would say. Did she dare? She did.

> Hey. Is the limo and stuff confirmed for the prom?-J

This was a good sign. Wasn't it? Unless he'd decided he wasn't going to the prom and wanted her to cancel everything. Only one way to find out. She muttered to herself that it wasn't easy to type a text with your fingers crossed.

> Yes. We're all set to go for the big day!-T

> Good. Just thought I'd check.-J

> xo-T

Teal let out the sigh she had been holding in that she hadn't been aware of. So far so good. They were still going to the prom.

***

Teal's father took Violet from Teal.

"You excited about your trip?" he asked. "It's coming up right after the prom, isn't it?"

"I can hardly sleep sometimes. Can't believe everything that's going on. Prom. The trip. College."

"We'd love to see you before you leave for your trip. How about I pick you up the night before you head out?

Then, if you like, you can spend the night here and we can take you to the airport? That way, everybody'll get to see you before you leave. How's that sound?"

Teal had figured this would have been the last time she'd see them all before she left, but if he wanted to see her one more time again, that was fine by her.

"Sure, Dad, that would be great."

The phone buzzed. Teal looked down to see who it was. A message from Jackson. Teal quickly checked it.

> Can we meet up?-J
>
> Sure. When?-T
>
> Now? I could come over to your place?-J
>
> I can't. –T
>
> But you just said sure. Why can't you? Where are you?-J
>
> I thought you meant later today. Or maybe tomorrow.-T
>
> I thought maybe we could talk.-J
>
> Okay. Go ahead.-T
>
> I don't want to do it through text, Teal. In person.-J

This did not sound good. Teal didn't want to meet up with Jackson now. Whatever he wanted to talk about couldn't be good. Not if he wanted to do it in person. Not to mention he'd seemed very persistent.

> I'm spending the night at my dad's.-T
>
> Okay. I'll come over there.-J

Since she wasn't sure what he had to say, Teal thought maybe it wasn't the best idea for Jackson to come to her father's place. Her father liked him and all, but she wasn't sure what was going on.

> How about I meet you at the Second Cup close to Dad's?-T
>
> I can be there in a half hour.-J
>
> I was thinking more tonight. Like around 8 pm?-T
>
> I guess.-J
>
> Sounds good. See you later. xo-T
>
> kk-J

Now Teal was definitely worried. This wasn't the Jackson she knew. What was so important that he had to talk to her tonight? If he was excited about something, he sure as heck didn't seem like it. She checked the time and it was only 3 pm. She still had a couple of hours to go until supper, and then get through the meal, and then play with the kids for a bit and then it would be their bedtime and then after all that, it would be time to go meet Jackson. And then. And then. And then. It was going to be a long day.

She tried to keep busy. She read more books to Toby than she could keep track of. That helped some. She spent a lot of time with the baby.

Then finally, it was time to meet with Jackson.

52

Teal arrived before Jackson did so the waiting made her tension worse. But when he got there, she hugged him, noting that nothing seemed unusual. Good sign.

She waited. He was the one who wanted to meet up. He should start the conversation.

"Thanks for agreeing to meet me here." He smiled, but somehow it wasn't the same.

"Welcome." Whatever he had to say to her, she had no desire to make it easier on him.

"Here it is, Teal. I am just going to come right out and say it."

Teal inhaled a deep breath and let it out slowly. She had to stay composed.

"I just don't get why I can't come with you on the trip. How come you don't want me to come with you?" He actually looked sad.

Teal shrugged. She took a moment before speaking.

The last thing she wanted to do was make things worse by saying stuff she didn't mean just because she was upset.

"It has nothing to do with you, Jackson. I just want to go alone. This is what Miss Tate wanted. For me to experience freedom. For me to go and see *my* house by *my*self. To go and explore just a sliver of this world before I head off to college."

"You still need to make a choice about college."

"I have made my choice. I put in my acceptance today."

"That's great," Jackson said, smiling. "I'm happy for you! What have you decided?"

"I'll be the taking the Social Work Program. The three-year one at Algonquin. My specialty for my third year will be working with seniors."

Her parents knew she'd made that decision and so did Olive, but Teal herself was still in shock. It felt nice to brag. She'd worked hard and it had paid off.

Now for the hard part. Teal needed to just put it out there. Say it now. Get it over with.

"If it's over between us just because you can't come with me on my trip, then I'm sorry it has to be that way. I thought I knew you better than that." She looked down at the floor, not trusting herself not to cry.

"What are you talking about? I wasn't going to break up with you just because you won't let me tag along with you on your trip. That's ridiculous!"

She didn't know what to say. She hadn't seen him like this before.

"Am I upset? Yeah. Why? Because I'm going to miss

you. And I have to admit that I'm jealous." He grinned. "But that's it. I'm not going anywhere. I'll be right here waiting when you get back." He grasped her hand and squeezed it.

What a relief. She was lucky to have him.

"One more thing we need to talk about, though. The prom."

Oh, she'd almost forgotten about that. Well, not the prom itself, but the after part. How was she going to deal with that? She cared for Jackson—there was no doubt about that—but she didn't believe she was ready to share her entire self with him yet.

"Okay. What about it?"

"Our parents know we're going to the prom. They know we didn't do anything special for mine last year. I'm not sure what your mother thinks but my mom's afraid I might do something stupid at a party after the prom. You know."

Teal knew.

"Therefore, she has come up with a compromise. She knows I can go to a hotel or whatever." He paused as though he were looking for the right word, wanting to make sure the next part came out right.

Ha! He's been thinking about getting a hotel!

Cripes. Now what was she going to do? She didn't trust herself to go to a hotel. There would be even more pressure.

"Teal? You listening?"

"Yeah. Yes, I am."

"So Mom suggested that instead of us being who-knows-where at all hours of the night, that you spend the night at my place instead. And don't worry, Mom won't be there."

Teal raised her eyebrows in a question. So the plan was for her to go and spend the night at Jackson's after Prom and his mother would disappear for the night? Where would his mother go? And did she have any chance at all of her own mother agreeing to this plan?

"Where's your mom going to go? I'm not sure my mother will agree to this."

"Our mothers have already talked about it. Not going to lie to you. At first, your mom said no, flat out. Then I guess my mom explained to her all the stuff we could be doing elsewhere, unsupervised, with a bunch of other people who may or may not be as well-behaved as we are. Then she agreed."

"She did?" A laugh burst out of Teal. "You have to be kidding me!"

"Yep. It will be just you and me. I swear, no pressure. It'll be nice with neither of us having to leave for curfew."

Teal was still nervous but at least she wouldn't have to battle a hotel scene. She knew her way home from Jackson's. Just in case.

53

The perfect song to end the dance was "I'll Never Love Again" by Lady Gaga. The limo ride had been awesome. Olive had found a date at the last minute and she and her date seemed to have hit it off. This was good. Teal knew Olive was trying to keep her mind busy.

They had taken photo upon photo using props, all kinds of silly things to mark this special occasion. An occasion that should be marked and remembered.

Teal had no idea what Olive was doing after the actual prom itself, but figured it was none of her business.

As far as Teal herself was concerned, she was nervous about things to come later on in the evening between Jackson and her, of course, but she was looking forward to it. Teal could hardly believe she was actually done with high school. She had graduated. She was moving on to the next phase of her life: college. She had so much to look forward to. It was hard to believe that only a year ago, she was having a hard time seeing the tunnel, let alone the light at the end of it.

***

As soon as they entered Jackson's house, the butterflies let loose in Teal's stomach. Jackson had said many times that there would be no pressure; just the two of them, and it would be nice and quiet.

The pull-out couch was already set up with lots of pillows, and on the coffee table was a bunch of small candles all lined up. Everything was cozy and inviting.

"So far so good?" Jackson asked.

Teal tossed him a relieved smile. "So far so good."

"There's a fruit and cheese plate in the fridge and some other munchies on the kitchen counter."

Teal opened the fridge. Inside was the platter and plenty of options for drinks as well: sparkling water, four kinds of pop, two different juices and a Caesar 4-pack. On the kitchen counter were four bags of chips.

"Do you think we have enough stuff to eat tonight?" Teal laughed.

"Yeah," said Jackson. "She went a bit overboard. But for breakfast, all you get is coffee or tea and a muffin. Just a head's up about that." He pulled her into his arms. They kissed. Twice.

Earlier that week they had discussed what they might wear to bed. Going to bed fully clothed seemed somewhat silly. Especially since they didn't know when they would have another chance at a night to themselves like this. It hadn't taken them long to come to the conclusion that even the *idea* of going to bed completely naked would make them both uncomfortable.

In the end, Jackson suggested he wear pajama bottoms and she wear one of his T-shirts as a nightgown. He had promised no pressure, and true to form, Jackson kept his word.

In no time, they were cuddled together on the pull-out couch, watching one of Teal's all-time-favorite movies, *The Goonies*.

Knowing it was one of her faves, Jackson had bought a copy just so they could watch it together on their special night. Thinking of how Jackson was always thoughtful where she was concerned, made her smile.

Her happy sigh prompted Jackson to ask, "Is everything all right?"

"I'm just so happy right now, Jackson. Everything feels right. It's hard to explain."

"I'm glad." He kissed her lips then brushed her cheek.

Teal pointed at the TV. "This is the character I was talking about. They call him Chunk."

Jackson turned his attention back to *The Goonies*.

***

An hour into the movie, Teal was startled by a snore. She turned to find Jackson asleep beside her, his arm thrown over her stomach. She wriggled slightly, hoping to wake him up, but it didn't work.

When the movie was over, she turned off the TV and blew out the last candle. And that was the end of their evening.

Teal wasn't certain if she were irritated or relieved that Jackson had fallen asleep during their special evening. Was she irritated because she'd anticipated the two of them staying up chatting, fooling around and watching movies till the sun came up? That's how special nights ended in the movies, wasn't it? Was she relieved because she hadn't had to make the big decision about going all the way with Jackson? Had the choice been made for her? No. She could have tried harder to wake him, couldn't she? That had to be a sign that she was, in fact, *not* ready. Wasn't it?

54

THE DAY HAD FINALLY ARRIVED. After all the plans and counting down she had done, it was here. Teal was about to start another chapter in her life. Alone. And she couldn't wait.

Teal's father threw his arm over her shoulder and said, "How about a picture like this, Jackson? With Teal in the middle." To Teal, he said, "You have to be in the middle or else the picture won't look right."

Teal rolled her eyes. She had to pose for yet another picture? She inhaled deeply, but her mother raised her eyebrows at her, so she let the breath out slowly and with a sheepish grin.

A few more photos, some more goodbyes, and that would be it. A few minutes of annoyance for a month of freedom. *I can handle this.*

It seemed weird to see her parents together. They'd both attended her high school graduation, but still, it was something that would take getting used to. She supposed it would have been easier without Tonya being there with Toby and Violet, but they were all present.

More than anything, she appreciated that Jackson had switched shifts at the computer store he was working at so he could say goodbye to her at the airport.

She'd told him not to bother. That her whole family—*both* families—would be there so it would just be annoying anyway. He'd said okay, but then he'd showed up at the last minute. Teal had been surprised and glad at the same time.

Teal hugged her mother goodbye first. They hadn't been spending a lot of time together lately and she felt somewhat guilty about that, but she wasn't a high-school kid anymore, was she? She promised herself she'd send a postcard shortly after her arrival in Spain. She'd say something sweet, or maybe she'd send flowers, just because.

Next, her father. They'd become closer than when her parents were together. This was probably due to all the changes in his life and his wanting to include Teal in it that had brought them together more. She'd miss him. And his yummy pancakes.

Tonya hugged her and smiled. It was hard to believe that at one point, Teal hadn't wanted Tonya to be a part of her life. If it weren't for Tonya, Teal wouldn't have Toby, or Violet. Right now, she couldn't imagine her life without Toby or the baby.

Teal bent down to give her little brother a high-five. "Remember what Daddy's supposed to practice making while I'm gone?"

"Pancake!" Toby clapped his hands and lunged forward to hug Teal.

Teal closed her eyes. The tears were there. Right there fighting to be released, but she wouldn't let them. Not now. Not in front of everybody.

She picked Toby up and squeezed him gently. She'd miss the others, sure she would, but she was certain she'd miss Toby the most. And Jackson! But there was no way she would ever say anything like that out loud.

Next, she held Violet for a moment, staring down at the sweet innocent bundle in her arms. She kissed her forehead before she passed her back to Tonya. No doubt Violet would look different, maybe even be making her first cooing baby talk sounds by the time Teal returned from her trip.

Jackson grabbed her hands in his and everyone else stepped back to give them space. He kissed each of her hands then their eyes locked. Teal was having even greater difficulty holding her tears back.

"This is it," he said. "What you've been waiting for. Go for it. But be careful, okay?" He grinned then kissed her quickly on the lips.

Teal bowed her head. This was it. She held her head high as she smiled at everyone. They had closed the gap again and were all crowded around her once more.

"Goodbye. I'll miss you lots, but I'll be in touch soon as I can. I'll be home to bug you all before you know it!"

Teal was scared and nervous and she knew everybody knew she was, but she still didn't want to show it.

Then a familiar female voice: "Go for it!" It was Olive, yelling as she ran toward Teal. "You can do anything. *The scariest moment is always just before you start. After that, things can only get better.* Stephen King wrote that!" She swept Teal into a big hug.

"You made it!"

"I did, didn't I?" Olive said, all out of breath. "I had to see you before you left, silly. Don't forget me while you're gone, eh?"

As Teal walked backwards toward the line of travelers boarding her flight, Olive blew her a kiss.

"I won't," she called back, then turned toward the next chapter of her life.

This is it. She was ready.

Acknowledgments

WRITING A BOOK TAKES MORE than just an idea, time, and words. It takes patience, friends, and guidance from a team of people. I would like to thank Sherrill Wark, Phyllis Bohonis, Dakota Morgan, David Villeneuve, and Janice Nelson. Thank you for your time, thoughts, and encouragement.

About the Author

Photo by David Villeneuve

CATINA NOBLE IS A CANADIAN, MULTI-GENRE WRITER. Her work is eclectic and contains something for everyone. She has over two hundred publications including her books, short stories, poetry, and articles.

Her work has appeared in several publications, including, but not limited to: *Chicken Soup for the Soul*: "10 Keys to Happiness," *Woman's World Magazine, Bywords Magazine, Y Travel Blog, Canadian Newcomer Magazine, The Mindfulword, Perceptive Travel* and many others.

In 2013, her poem "You Can't See Me" won first place in the Canadian Author's Association, National Capital Region's poetry contest.

Four of her books: *Finding Evie, Vacancy at the Food Court & Other Short Stories, Everest Base Camp: Close Call*, and *I'm Glad I Didn't Kill Myself* have won the Reader's Favorite 5-Star, Silver Seal of approval.

Catina Noble has a B.A. in Psychology from Carleton University and a Social Services Worker Diploma from Algonquin College.

She currently writes, works full time and is enrolled in the Addictions & Mental Health program at Algonquin College.

Her favorite place to write is at a local coffee shop. Sometimes her dog, Aspen, and cat, PJ, supervise the creative writing process.

Other Books by Catina Noble

Letter Rip (2022)
The Happily Ever After? (2022)
Finding Evie (2022)
Cat's Journals: *El Camino on a Wrecked Ankle* (2020)
Cat's Journals: *Everest Base Camp: Close Call* (2020)
This Is It (2019)
Not Again (2019)
Cat's Journals: *Lost at 13* (2019)
Not Just Me (2018)
Cat's Journals: *I'm Glad I Didn't Kill Myself* (2016)
Vacancy at the Food Court & Other Short Stories (2016)
Katzenjammer (2015)

www.ingramcontent.com/pod-product-compliance
Lightning Source LLC
Chambersburg PA
CBHW071653090426
42738CB00009B/1509